Better Homes and Gardens®

BEAUTIFUL EMBROIDERY

MURDOCH BOOKS®
Sydney • London • Vancouver • New York

Contents

Potpourri

NICHOLAS
BABY

Silken rose sachets and shoe stuffers

Ribbon-embroidered roses, colonial knot forget-me-knots and seed pearls are massed together to decorate the sachets.

Decorated daintily with white and yellow roses, tiny blue forget-me-nots, and subtle seed pearls, these sachets and shoe stuffers are as useful as they are beautiful.

Finished size Hosiery sachet approximately 17 x 16 cm; handkerchief sachet approximately 25 x 19 cm; shoe stuffers approximately 13 x 13 cm

Stitches

Colonial knot

Detached chain stitch

Materials

- 85 cm of white satin
- 70 cm of white taffeta lining
- Rajmahal art silk in blue (211)
- DMC Coton Perlé no. 8 in white
- 17 m of 8 mm wide white silk ribbon
- 4 m of 3 mm wide pale yellow silk ribbon
- 8 m of 3 mm wide apple green silk ribbon
- 50 cm of 2 mm wide blue satin ribbon
- Tapestry needle size 24
- Crewel needle size 9
- 1 m of white satin piping
- 2.3 m of pearl beading
- 50 cm of 75 cm wide thin nylon wadding
- Two pearl buttons
- 2–3 packets of 3 mm seed pearls
- Small quantity of nylon stuffing
- White machine thread
- Tissue or greaseproof paper
- 15 cm (6 in) embroidery hoop
- HB pencil
- Ruler and scissors

LEFT Keep your shoes, hosiery and handkerchiefs in perfect condition with these stunning sachets and shoe stuffers.

HOSIERY AND HANDKERCHIEF SACHETS

Both sachets are made in the same way. These instructions are for the smaller sachet, with the measurements for the large size in brackets.

EMBROIDERY

1 Cut a piece of satin 22 x 8 cm (30 x 8 cm). On the reverse side, with an HB pencil, rule up a strip 18 x 3 cm wide (25 x 3 cm) centred on the satin. Using sewing thread, hand baste along the pencil lines.

2 On the right side of the satin mark the position of each spider's web rose by placing a series of dots in a circle approximately 1 cm in diameter. Place the dots at 12, 2, 5, 7 and 10 o'clock. Scatter the roses along the strip (see the photograph above). Using a crewel needle and Coton Perlé, work a five-legged evenly spaced frame by stitching from the back of the fabric in the 12 o'clock position, back down through the centre, then up at 7 o'clock, then back down through the centre, and so on through 5, 10 and 2 o'clock (see the diagram on page 6).

3 Using the 8 mm white silk ribbon, thread the tapestry needle, pass the needle through the tail (see the diagram below) and pull gently until the ribbon sits flat at the end of the needle (that is, so there is no bulk). Leaving approximately 1 cm of ribbon at the back of the work, bring the needle up between two of the Perlé threads and as close as possible to the centre of the circle. The ribbon does not pass through the satin again until the rose is complete.

4 Starting at the centre and working anti-clockwise, pass the ribbon over the first Perlé thread, then under the second and over the third. Pull the ribbon up gently and repeat until the frame is totally covered and the rose is complete. When done, pass the needle under the rose and through the satin, leaving a 1 cm tail as before. (Alternatively, you could leave the ribbon threaded and pass from one rose to the next, beginning each rose in the 12 o'clock position.) The tails on the back will be caught down when the other embroidery and the pearls are added. Use the 3 mm pale yellow ribbon for a few of the roses.

5 In the spaces around the roses, work leaves in detached chain stitch, using the apple green silk ribbon and leaving room for the colonial knots (forget-me-nots) and pearls. Then using two strands of the blue (211) Rajmahal silk in the crewel needle, work colonial knots among the roses and leaves.

ASSEMBLING THE SACHET

1 Pin the piping along the embroidery and carefully hand baste (this stitching should lie over the previous basting used as the embroidery guide).

2 Cut a strip of satin 21 x 6.5 cm wide (27 x 7 cm) and a rectangle of satin 46 x 21 cm (55 x 27 cm). With right sides together, baste a 21 cm (27 cm) side of each of these pieces to either side of the piping, taking a 1.5 cm seam allowance. Using a zipper foot, carefully stitch through the thicknesses along each side of the embroidery, ensuring the needle is going into the material as close as possible to the piping. Trim the seams to 1 cm and finger press the seam allowance towards the embroidered band.

3 Add the seed pearls to the embroidery but don't stitch them too close to the ends of the embroidery as they may get in the way when stitching the side seams. You can always add a couple after you have stitched the seams.

Working a frame for the rose

Threading the ribbon

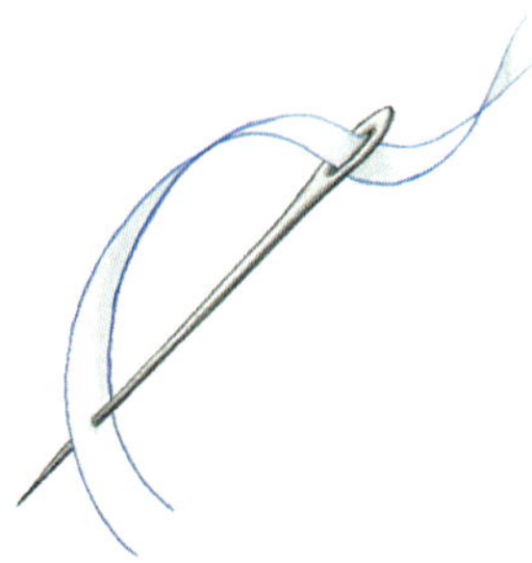

Making up the sachet

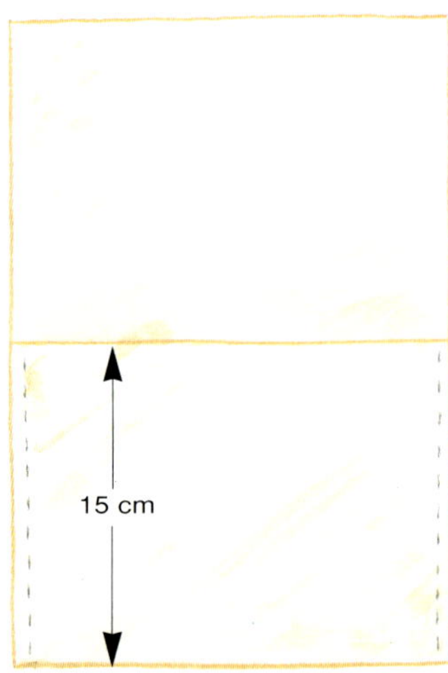

This beautiful satin sachet is lined in taffeta and edged with pearl beading. Place a sprig of lavender inside for a sweet fragrance.

A thin, blue satin ribbon sewn to the top of these luxurious shoe stuffers accentuates the blue of the forget-me-nots.

4 Cut a piece of thin nylon wadding the same size as the sachet and hand baste this to the wrong side. Fold the end of the sachet opposite the embroidery 15 cm (18 cm) onto the wrong side and machine stitch down each side (see diagram opposite). Trim the seams and turn right side out.
5 Cut a piece of satin 20.5 x 14.5 cm (27.5 x 19.5 cm). Fold one of the short ends under 1.5 cm and press. Take the other short end and align the raw edge to the end of the embroidered flap, right sides together. Machine stitch along the sides and across the top. Trim the seams and corners; turn right side out.
6 Cut a piece of taffeta lining 34 x 20.5 cm (38 x 27.5 cm) . With right sides together stitch the top edge of the lining to the other end of the satin envelope. Fold the opposite end of the lining in 1.5 cm and press. Then join the edges of the lining so that the right sides are facing, and stitch along the sides to form a 15 cm (18 cm) deep bag. Trim the seams. Anchor the lining bag to the satin envelope with a few small stitches through the seam allowance. Turn through to the right side. Slip stitch the satin flap lining to the folded edge of the lining bag.

TO FINISH

Hold the sachet face down with its flap open. Starting at the bottom of the right-hand side of the sachet, couch (oversew) the pearl beading into the crease of the side seams continuing up the right-hand side of the flap, across the flap and down the left-hand side, stitching between each pearl. Stitch a pearl button in the centre of the front, just below the edge of the flap and work a buttonhole loop on the flap.

SHOE STUFFERS

1 Trace the two patterns (see page 104) onto tissue or greaseproof paper. Cut each pattern from satin making sure the grain lines are correct. You will need four uppers and two soles to make a pair.
2 Take a 5 mm seam allowance and machine stitch the centre seams of the uppers. Work the embroidery in the same way as for the sachets, but follow the design below. Stitch the seed pearls among the embroidered roses.
3 With right sides together, machine stitch the sole to the uppers leaving approximately 5 cm across the top end to turn the stuffer through. Using a gathering stitch setting on your machine, stitch across the top edge of the uppers about 5 mm from the edge.
4 Turn through to the right side and pack nylon stuffing firmly into each shoe stuffer. Pull up the gathering threads and turn under a 5 mm seam allowance. Stitch together across the top of each stuffer, adjusting the gathers.
5 Starting from a top corner, couch pearl beading around each stuffer, stitching between each pearl for the best results. Tie two small blue ribbon bows and stitch into position on each stuffer.

Shoe stuffer design

Cross-stitch picture mount and box lid

Neat geometric designs and cross stitch are a perfect combination.

The inspirational designs on this picture mount and box lid have been largely based on the tiles of Federation homes. With their soft, yet vibrant colours, these items will suit every home.

Finished size Picture mount 20 x 30 cm; embroidery for box lid 11.5 x 12 cm (maximum)

Stitches

Cross stitch

Materials

- 30 cm of 28-count ecru linen
- DMC Flower Thread: blue (2827), yellow (2446), red (2303), green (2732)
- Tapestry needle size 24
- 25 cm of pellon
- Picture frame 30 x 20 cm, with 4.5 cm wide surround
- Round box approximately 15 cm in diameter
- Medium weight cardboard
- Dental floss
- PVA adhesive
- Fray Stop
- Fine braid or cord (optional)
- Fading ink fabric marker or HB pencil
- Scissors

PICTURE MOUNT

1 Cut a piece of linen 30 x 40 cm. Begin your cross stitch at a point 5 cm down and 5 cm in from the top left corner. Starting with green (2732) thread, work from left to right across the rows, referring to the chart on page 10 for colour changes.

2 Once the embroidery is complete, cut out the centre of the linen, allowing 1 cm for the seams. Press on the wrong side only.

3 Take the frame and paint or finish as desired. Trace out a cardboard template for the exact size of the area to be covered (including the middle cut-out section) and cut carefully. Place the template over the frame to ensure it is a perfect fit. Trim the outside and inside edges very slightly to allow the linen to cover the cardboard without extending beyond the frame.

4 Take the piece of pellon and, in one piece, glue it to the cardboard. Allow to dry, then trim it to match the cardboard exactly.

5 Position the embroidery on the cardboard to establish the outside and inside edges. Cut around the outside and inner edges, allowing a 1 cm seam allowance on all. Dab Fray Stop on the inside corners of the linen where it will later be cut to wrap around the cardboard.

6 Apply adhesive to the back of the cardboard only and glue down the two outside long edges of the embroidery first. Make sure the cross-stitch rows are an even distance from both edges. Glue down the two short ends in the same manner, being careful to fold the corners so that they lie flat and are neat. On the inside edges, cut into each corner with one cut (the Fray Stop you applied earlier will prevent fraying). Glue down the two long sides first, followed by the two short ends.

7 Spread adhesive evenly over the frame, going right into the edges and corners. Press the covered cardboard onto the frame, pressing down firmly and evenly all around.

RIGHT *Your favourite photograph and small treasures will be sitting pretty in this picture mount and box.*

Kodak

Picture mount chart

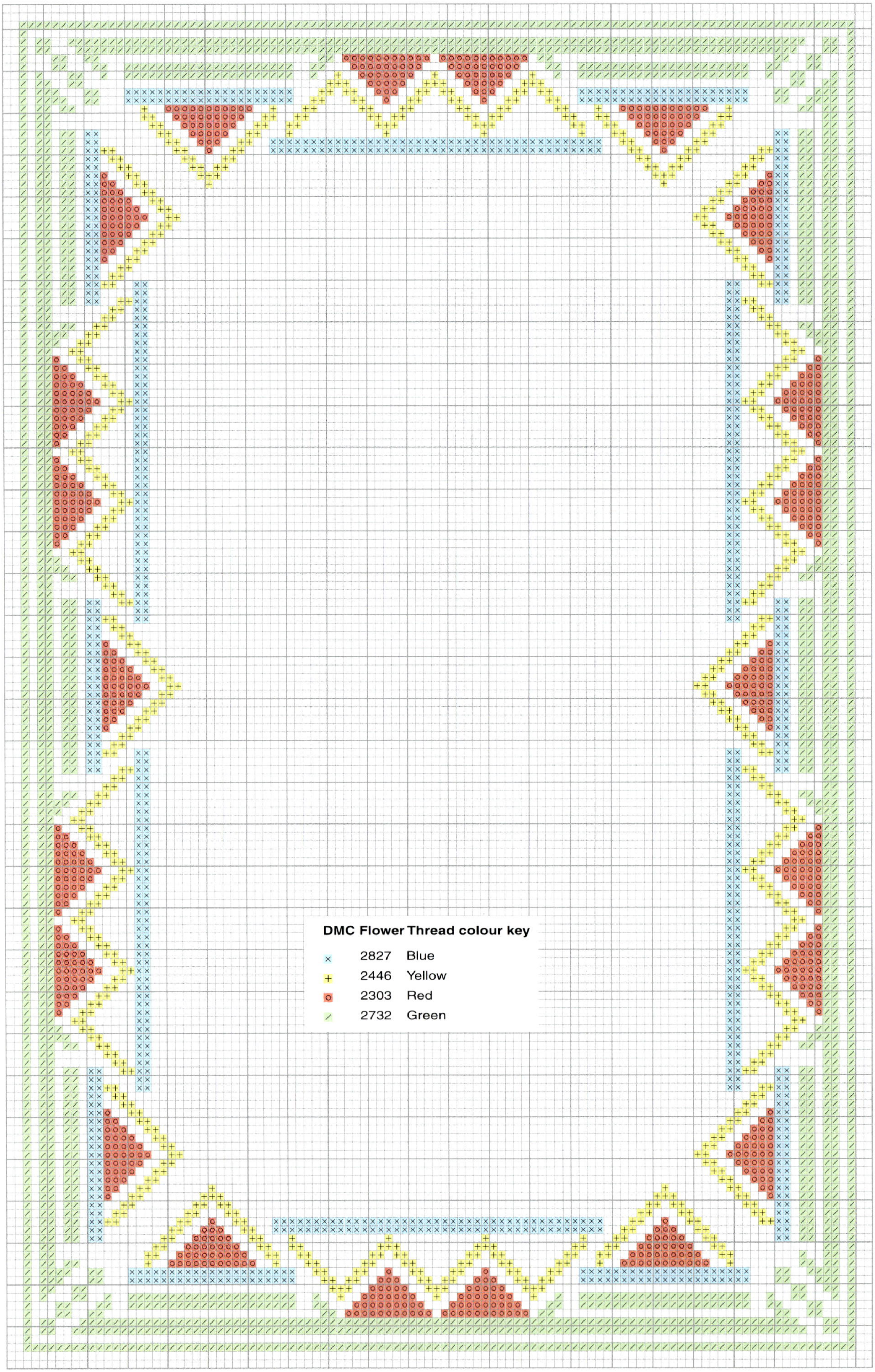

BOX LID

1 Cut a piece of linen 25 x 25 cm. Find the centre and count the stitches to the top of the design. Begin stitching here with blue (2827) thread, working from left to right and changing colour as specified on the chart. When done, press the wrong side only.

2 Paint or finish the box as desired. Trace out a cardboard template of the lid and cut carefully. Place it over the lid to ensure it is a good fit, then trim the edges slightly to allow the linen to cover the edge without extending beyond it.

3 Cut a circle of pellon the same size as the cardboard, spread adhesive onto the cardboard and press the pellon in place. Place this circle on the wrong side of the embroidery and mark around the edge with a fading ink pen or a very faint pencil line.

4 Use dental floss to tack a row of stitches 5 mm out from the marked line, then trim the linen 5 mm away from these stitches. Place the embroidery over the pellon and pull the dental floss to gather the linen over the cardboard. Tighten and secure the thread. Apply adhesive to the cardboard, and flatten out as many of the gathers as possible.

5 Cover the box lid evenly with adhesive and press the embroidery down firmly on top. If you want to neaten the edges, glue a fine braid or cord all around.

Box lid chart

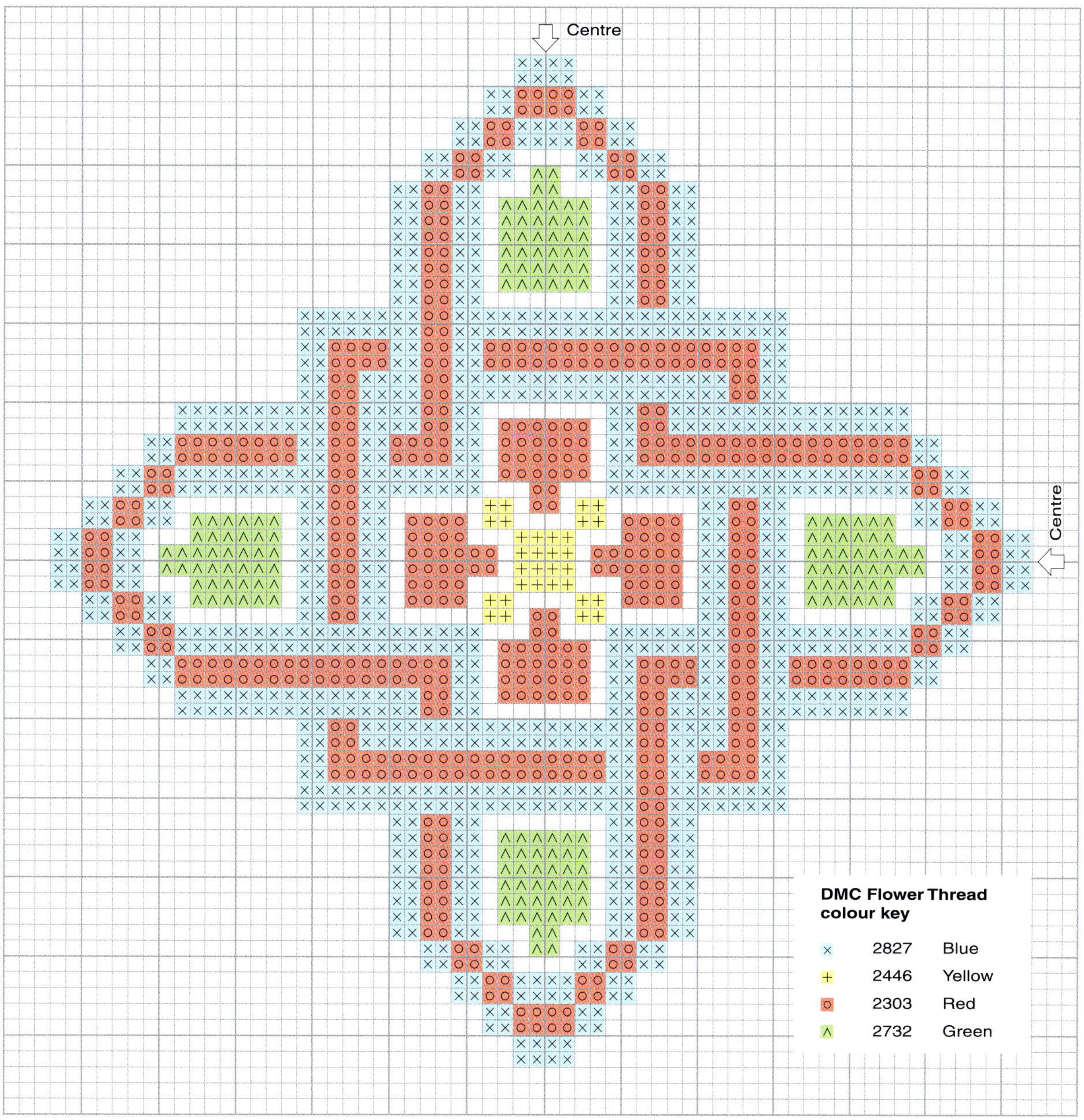

Country style table setting

The rich, brilliant colours of nature's garden are brought to life in this delightful table setting that is sure to receive lots of admiration. Deep yellow, red, purple, orange and various shades of green are combined to create an impressive effect.

Finished size Placemat 45 x 33 cm; napkin 33 x 33 cm; napkin ring 4 x 17 cm

Stitches

Chain stitch
Fly stitch
Hem stitch
Long and short stitch
Rosette chain stitch
Split stitch
Stem stitch

Materials

- 40 cm of ecru linen at least 100 cm wide
- DMC Coton à Broder in ecru
- DMC stranded embroidery cotton: yellow-green (3347), forest green (987), light avocado green (472), medium avocado green (470), dark avocado green (469), light pistachio green (369), dark pistachio green (320), jade (563), red (666), pale yellow (744), medium yellow (743), light mocha brown (3782), light beige-brown (543), golden brown (975)
- Madeira embroidery floss: orange (0203), purple (0714)
- 4 x 17 cm strip of iron-on vilene
- Crewel needle size 9 or 10
- Small button
- Scissors
- HB pencil

LEFT A variety of stitches and cottons are used to enhance the look of these charming vegetables, while the hem stitched border adds the final touch.

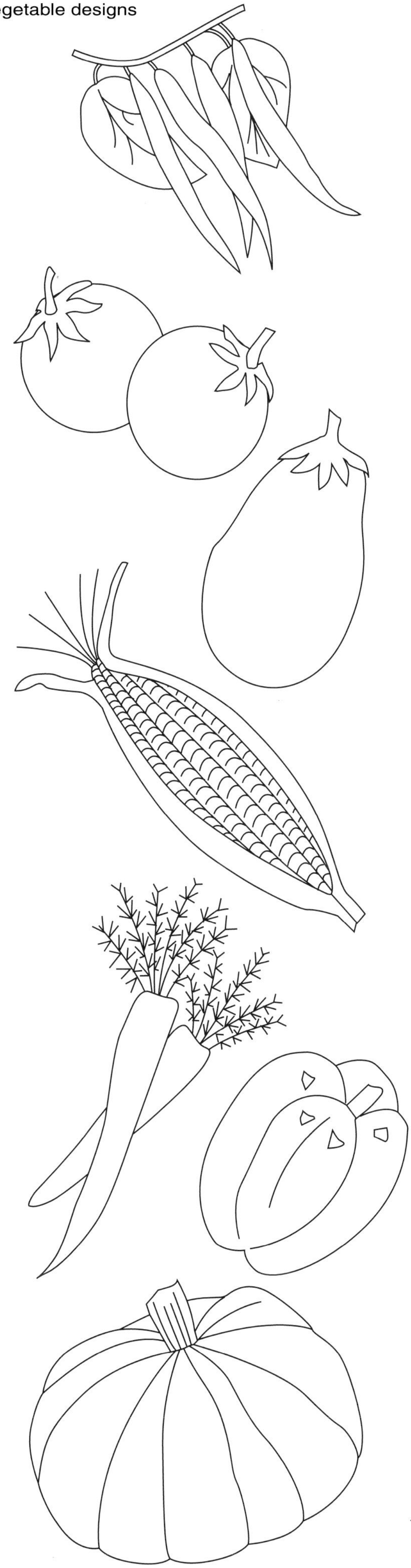

PLACEMAT AND NAPKIN

1 Cut two pieces of linen: 51 x 38 cm for the placemat and 38 x 38 cm for the napkin.
2 Turn and baste a 2.5 cm wide hem all around.
3 Withdraw three threads all around inside the hem, leaving a few centimetres at each end so the ends can be stitched into the back of the hem.
4 Use the Coton à Broder to hem stitch all around, catching the hem as you sew.
5 Transfer the vegetable motifs onto the left side of the placemat and the carrot motif onto one corner of the napkin and embroider according to the instructions below.

NAPKIN RING

1 Cut a piece of linen 19 x 19 cm.
2 Transfer the tomatoes motif to the centre of the linen, and work the embroidery according to the instructions below.
3 About 1 cm from each side of the embroidered motif, withdraw three threads and work hem stitch over them.
4 Place the strip of iron-on vilene across the back of the embroidery. Turn the edges in and stitch by hand using the Coton à Broder. Fold the top and bottom in over the vilene and stitch in place.
5 Work a buttonhole loop on one end and sew a button 1.5 cm from the edge of the other end.

EMBROIDERY

Beans: Use two strands of medium avocado green (470) for the outlines of the leaves and for the stems, working the leaves in chain stitch and the stems in stem stitch. Work the veins in the leaves with one strand of cotton in stem stitch. Use two strands of dark avocado green (469) to work the beans in chain stitch.

Tomatoes: Work in long and short stitch, using two strands of red (666) for the body and two strands of forest green (987) for the stems and calyx.

Aubergine: Work in stem stitch, using purple (0714) Madeira embroidery floss for the body and two strands of dark pistachio green (320) for the stem. The calyx is worked in long and short stitch.

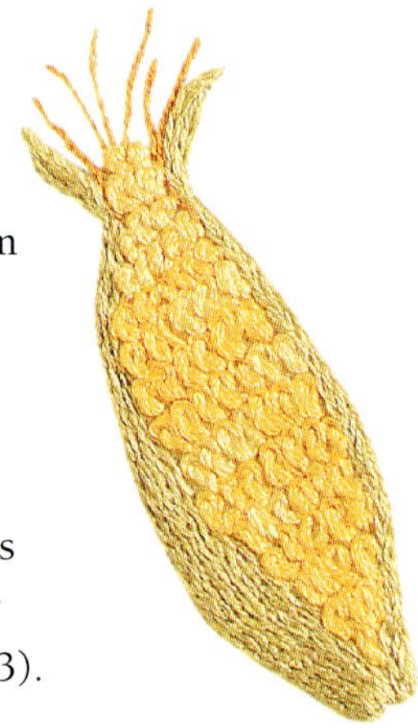

Corn: Use two strands of light avocado green (472) for the husk, working in stem stitch. The cornsilk is stitched in stem stitch using two strands of golden brown (975). For the kernels, work in rosette chain stitch with three strands of cotton and, as you move across the rows, alternate pale yellow (744) and medium yellow (743).

Carrots: Use orange (0203) Madeira embroidery floss for the carrots, working in stem stitch. Work the stems in stem stitch using two strands of medium avocado green (470) and use one strand of the same colour for working the leaves in fly stitch.

Capsicum: Work in long and short stitch using two strands of yellow-green (3347) for the body and two strands of forest green (987) for the stem. Add highlights of one strand of light avocado green (472) to the top of the capsicum.

Pumpkin: Outline the pumpkin with two rows of stem stitch using two strands of jade (563), then fill it in with split stitch using two strands of light pistachio green (369). For the stem use one strand each of light mocha brown (3782) and light beige-brown (543) and work in stem stitch.

Miniature tapestry pictures

The vibrant colours and geometric shapes used in these designs will give an edge to any decorative style.

These miniature tapestry pictures are a delight to make and beautiful to look at. Inspired by designs of the Victorian period, they will produce a stunning effect placed together on a mantelpiece or wall.

Finished size Approximately 4 cm square

Stitches

Continental stitch

Materials

- Three 10 cm squares of 18-count tapestry canvas
- Madeira Decora embroidery rayon: mid-blue (1495), lime green (1580), jade (1445), forest green (1570), cranberry (1583), rose (1508), straw (1466), dark red (1439), chartreuse (1448), bright orange-red (1437), dark lemon (1525)
- Tapestry needle size 22
- Masking tape
- Steam iron
- Piece of board (for example, a chopping board)
- Pegs
- Pencil
- Ruler

EMBROIDERY

1 Bind the edges of the canvas squares with masking tape. This will protect the rayon thread from catching on the rough edges of the canvas while you are working the embroidery.

2 Find the centre of the design you will be embroidering and diagonally count the number of stitches required from the centre to the top left-hand corner of the design.

3 Find the centre of the canvas and count diagonally to the left in a similar manner until you reach the number of stitches required. This gives you the starting point for the embroidery.

4 Using three strands of rayon and following the chart, work the design in continental stitch. Do not use any knots in this type of embroidery. Leave a tail of rayon behind your work, long enough so that, when the embroidery has been established, you can thread it up and slide it through a minimum of five stitches. End off in the same way.

BLOCKING

1 When the tapestry is complete, turn it onto the wrong side and press with a steam iron, allowing the steam to penetrate the canvas. Moisten it enough so the canvas can be stretched to make a perfect square.

2 Take the piece of board and, using a pencil and ruler, mark a 10 cm square on it.

3 Keep applying steam to the embroidery and, using pegs to hold the canvas down onto the board, line up the sides of the canvas with the 10 cm square.

4 Allow the tapestry to dry out thoroughly, then frame as desired.

Picture 1

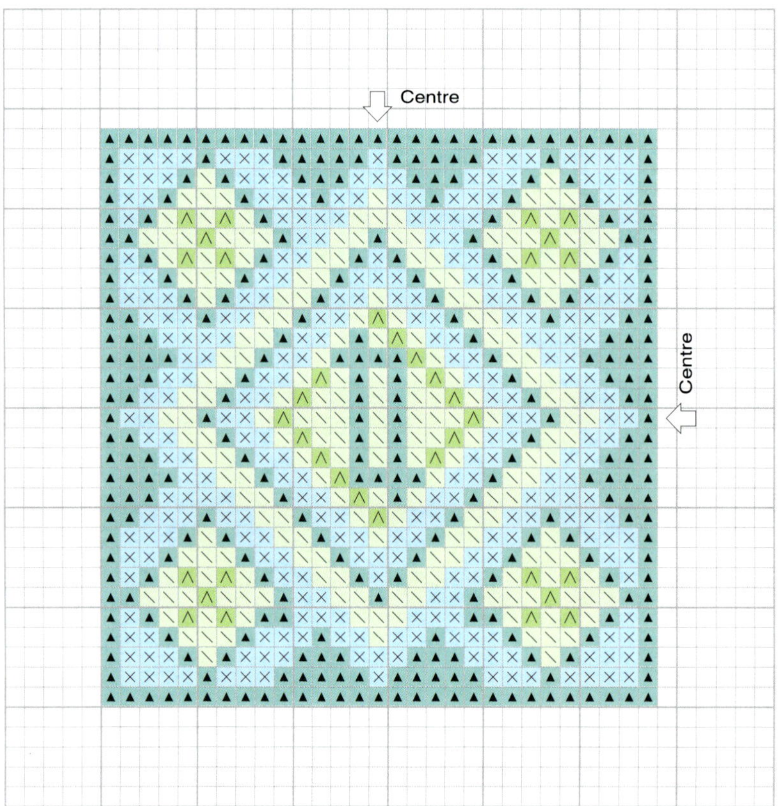

Madeira Decora embroidery rayon colour key

×	1495	Mid-blue
⟍	1580	Lime green
▲	1445	Jade
Λ	1570	Forest green

Picture 2

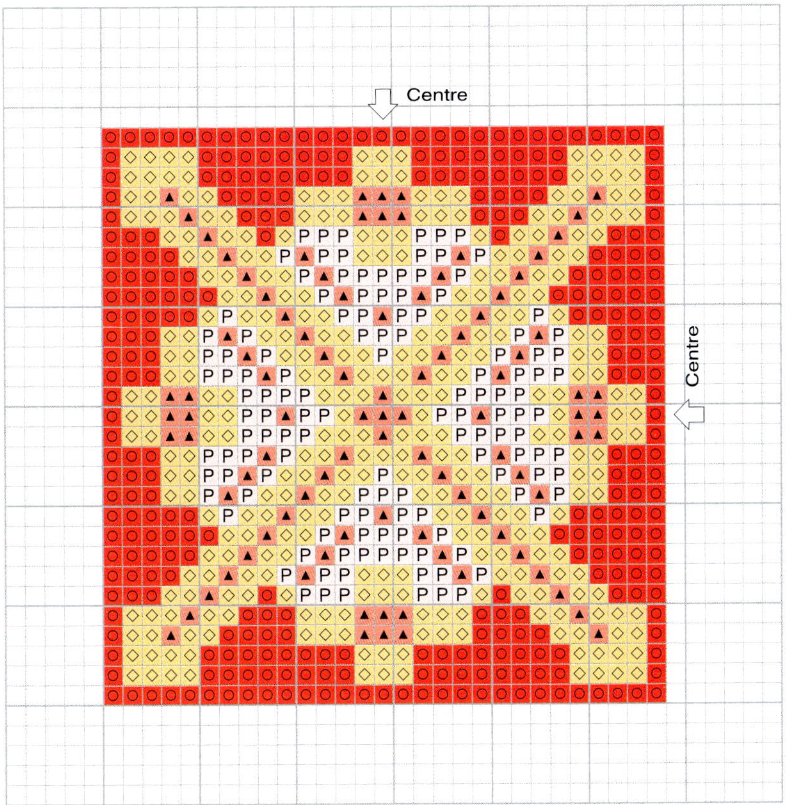

Madeira Decora embroidery rayon colour key

○	1439	Dark red
P	1508	Rose
◇	1466	Straw
▲	1583	Cranberry

Picture 3

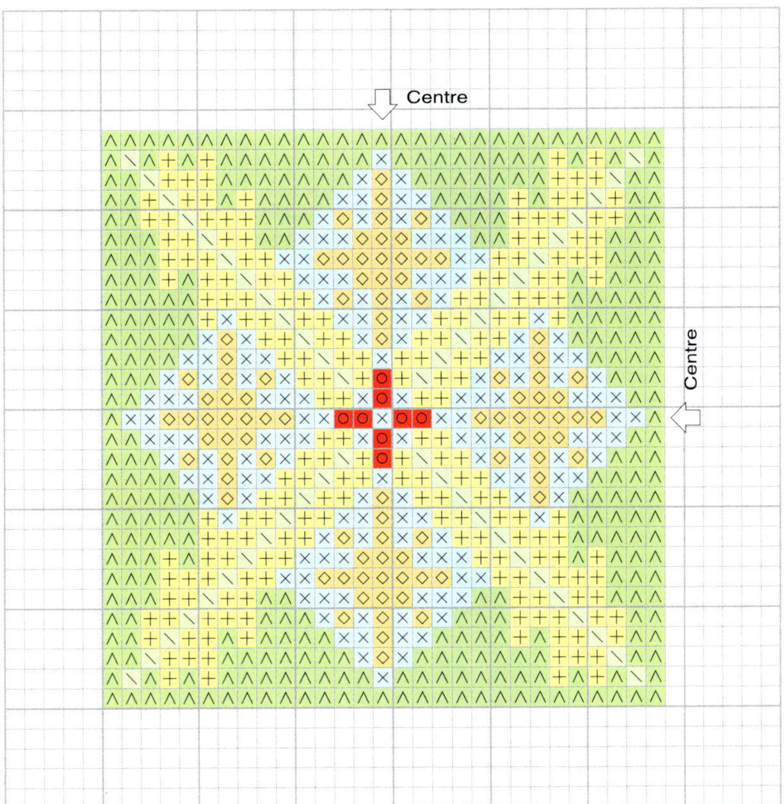

Madeira Decora embroidery rayon colour key

◇	1437	Bright orange-red
+	1525	Dark lemon
×	1495	Mid-blue
＼	1580	Lime green
∧	1448	Chartreuse
○	1439	Dark red

Grub roses for baby

A row of colonial knots at the centre of the design adds the final touch to this gorgeous arrangement of grub roses. This bib is perfect for baby to wear to special occasions, such as a christening.

Transform a plain white bib, singlet and pair of socks by embroidering charming grub rose motifs in soft pastel colours. Easy to make, these are guaranteed to make baby look adorable.

Finished size Bib motif 5.5 x 8 cm; socks motif 4.5 x 2 cm; singlet motif 5 x 3.5 cm

Stitches

Bullion stitch
Colonial knot
Stem stitch
Straight stitch

Materials

- Bib, singlet and socks
- DMC stranded embroidery cotton: light mauve (3689), baby pink (818), very light grey-green (928)
- Small piece of stiff tulle
- Straw needle pack size 3/9
- Water-erasable pen
- Blue or black permanent marker pen

LEFT This baby set has grub roses worked in bullion stitch using light mauve and baby pink cottons. The very light grey-green cotton used for the stems and leaves looks very delicate against the white background.

METHOD

1 Trace the main lines of each motif (see page 20) onto the piece of tulle using the permanent marker pen and allow it to dry. This is now your 'stencil' for positioning the motifs for embroidery.

2 Position the tulle on the corresponding item and mark the motif with the water-erasable pen. Work the embroidery as follows:

Stems. Use one strand of very light grey-green (928) cotton and work in stem stitch.

Leaves. Use one strand of very light grey-green (928) and work these in bullion stitch, giving the bottom half of the leaf twelve twists and the top fourteen. In order for the bullion to look like a leaf, place the second bullion slightly above the first, but back in the same hole at the base. Since it has a few more twists, it should curve slightly and give the illusion of a leaf shape.

Roses. Use two strands of cotton. For the centre, work two bullion stitches of eight wraps in light mauve (3689) cotton and for the outer circle work four

Socks motif

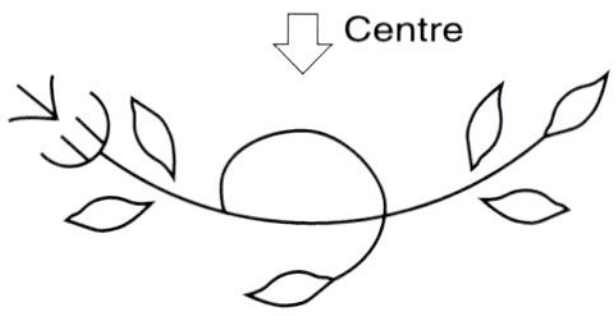

Bib motif

(optional)

Singlet motif

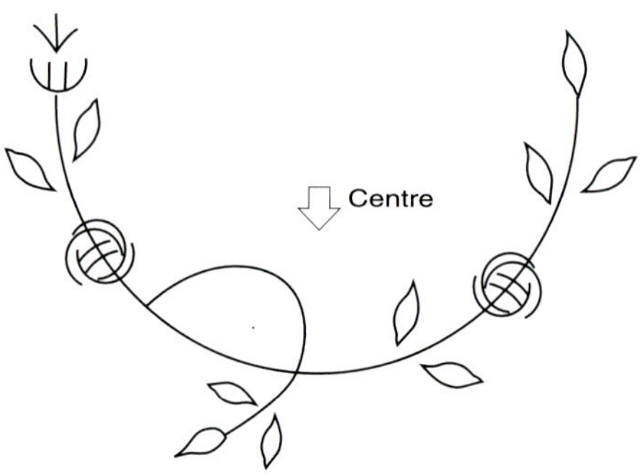

HINT

To keep bullion wraps in place while you're pulling the thread through, hold the wraps down with your thumb. If you find the wraps are quite tight and you have trouble pulling the needle through, give the needle a slight twist in the opposite direction to that of the wraps.

bullion stitches of eight wraps in baby pink (818). See the diagram on page 69.

Buds. Work the buds in two bullion stitches of eight wraps with two strands of light mauve (3689) cotton. Then with one strand of very light grey-green (928) cotton work the calyx in bullion stitch of sixteen wraps (see the diagram on page 69). Place the calyx along each side of the bud and finish it off with three small straight stitches at the tip of the buds.

3 For the bib, add four colonial knots in the centre of the design, worked with two strands of light mauve (3689) cotton. If your bib is suitable, work a small bud near the press stud fastening as has been done here.

4 When the embroidery is complete, use a damp cloth to gently remove the water-erasable pen marks.

A tiny bullion rose bud makes these plain white socks ultra special.

Assorted white handkerchiefs

Satin stitches are worked over small chain stitches to produce these pretty padded roses.

The delicate qualities of Richelieu cutwork, scalloped edges, hem stitching, and crochet with satin stitched roses are applied here to produce four dainty handkerchiefs to be proud of.

ROSE HANDKERCHIEF

Finished size Approximately 25 x 25 cm

Rose handkerchief design

Stitches

Chain stitch

Satin stitch

Materials

- Purchased cotton or linen handkerchief with edge suitable for crocheting (or use a handkerchief with crocheted edge, if preferred)
- DMC stranded embroidery cotton in white
- Coats Mercer crochet cotton no. 80 in white
- Crochet hook no. 06
- HB pencil

METHOD

1 Trace the outline of the rose design onto a corner of the handkerchief using the HB pencil.

2 Using two strands of embroidery cotton, pad each section of the design with small chain stitches, then work satin stitches being careful to cover the pencil outlines of the design.

3 Work the crochet edge using the crochet cotton and hook.

First row: work double crochet into each hole around the handkerchief.

Second row: 1 dc into the first dc, * 2 trebles 3 chain (slip stitch into first chain to form picot) and 2 trebles into next dc. Miss 1 dc, 1 dc into next dc. Repeat from * all around edge.

RICHELIEU HANDKERCHIEF

Finished size Approximately 30.5 x 30.5 cm

Stitches

Buttonhole stitch

Materials

- ◆ 35 cm square of handkerchief linen
- ◆ DMC stranded embroidery cotton in white
- ◆ DMC Coton Perlé no. 8 in white
- ◆ Crewel needle size 9
- ◆ White pure cotton machine thread
- ◆ Four 12 cm squares of calico
- ◆ 12 cm square of clear green self-adhesive covering
- ◆ 12 cm square of greaseproof paper
- ◆ Small, sharp-pointed embroidery scissors
- ◆ Tweezers
- ◆ HB pencil

Worked in one corner of the handkerchief, this charming design shows off the classic buttonhole bars of Richelieu cutwork.

METHOD

1 Square up the lines of the linen by removing a thread on each side. With the pencil, trace the design onto a corner of the linen, approximately 3 or 4 cm from the edges.

LEFT *Whether you keep these for yourself or give them to your friends as gifts, they are bound to become treasured favourites.*

2 Peel the backing paper off the self-adhesive covering and stick it to the greaseproof paper. Place the self-adhesive covering on top of the four calico squares and baste them together.

3 Place the corner of the linen with the design over the self-adhesive covering and baste through all the thicknesses. (This will hold the linen firmly in place while the buttonhole stitches are being worked, and

Richelieu handkerchief design

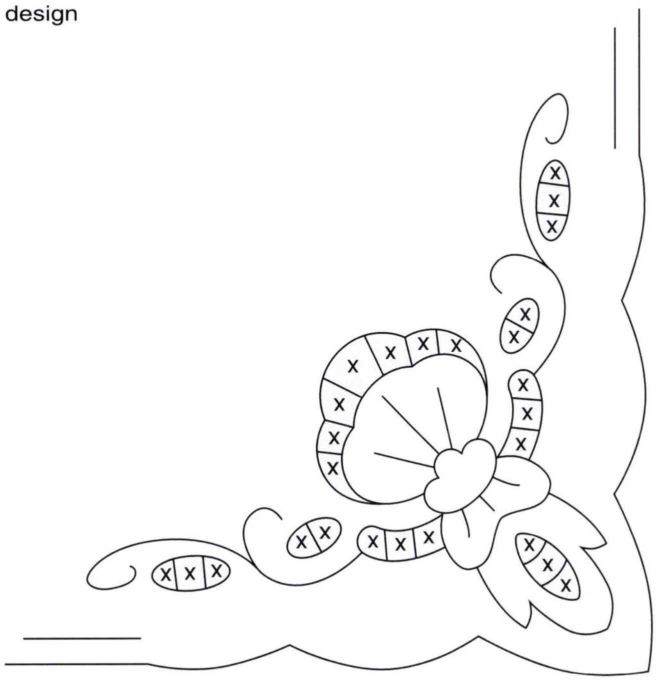

the self-adhesive covering will prevent your stitches going through to the calico.)

4 Using a small length of Coton Perlé and some machine thread with a knotted end, couch over all the lines that are to be buttonholed, using stitches 3–4 mm apart. Couch the scalloped edge, but do not couch over the bars.

5 Embroider the bars. Anchor one strand of cotton somewhere onto the design outline and form a bar. Work buttonhole stitch over the bar. Do not stitch through the linen.

6 Work buttonhole stitch over the couched threads, stitching into the linen but not through the self-adhesive covering and making sure you stitch into the end of the bars.

7 When the design is complete, remove the basting stitches by carefully snipping the stitches between the calico layers, then pull out the tiny basting threads with tweezers.

8 Beginning at each end of the scalloped edge, make a narrow hem, ensuring that it is even. On the right side of the handkerchief pull a single thread approximately 5 mm from the hem edge to guide the stitching.

9 With a very sharp-pointed pair of embroidery scissors cut away material from the outer edge of the scalloped corner and where indicated with an 'x' on the design, being very careful not to cut any bars.

SCALLOPED EDGE HANDKERCHIEF

Finished size Approximately 29 x 29 cm

Stitches

Buttonhole stitch
Chain stitch

Materials

- ◆ 34 cm square of handkerchief linen
- ◆ DMC stranded embroidery cotton in white
- ◆ Crewel needle size 9
- ◆ Small scissors
- ◆ HB pencil

METHOD

1 With the pencil, trace the scalloped edging all around the square of linen, making sure that the top of each scallop falls along the straight grain line and not right at the edge of the fabric.

Scalloped edge handkerchief design

2 Using two strands of white cotton, work chain stitch along the scallops (this will serve as padding for the buttonhole stitching to follow).

3 Work the scallops in buttonhole stitch. When stitching is completed, use a pair of sharp-pointed scissors to carefully cut around the scalloped edge.

A scalloped edge is simple to embroider. Trace the design near the fabric's edge, work in chain stitch, then again in buttonhole stitch, and trim. The result is a delicate, padded effect.

HEM STITCHED HANDKERCHIEF

Finished size Approximately 29 x 29 cm

Stitches

Hem stitch

Materials

- 30 cm square of handkerchief linen
- DMC stranded embroidery cotton in white
- Crewel needle size 9

METHOD

1 To ensure that the handkerchief is square and on true grain, measure each side and withdraw one or two threads from each side as the cutting line. Measure 1.5 cm in along each side and withdraw two or three threads for the hem stitch line.

2 Refer to the design. In one corner measure 2.5 cm in from each side and remove three threads from A to B, C to F, A to C, B to E, leaving enough of the thread to enable you to weave the ends back through the material for four or five threads. This will produce a square 3 x 3 cm with D to E and D to F extending 1 cm beyond the corner.

3 Measure 1.5 cm from each side of the square to find the centre G and remove three threads from G to H and G to I.

The effective design on this handkerchief is achieved by withdrawing linen threads, then working the lines in hem stitch.

4 Complete the corner design by working hem stitch along each of these lines, with one or two strands of cotton. Work the hem stitches around four threads and four threads below where the threads are pulled out.

5 Carefully press the hem in half. Baste if necessary, making sure the hem is even in width and hem stitch into the hem stitch line.

Hem stitched handkerchief design

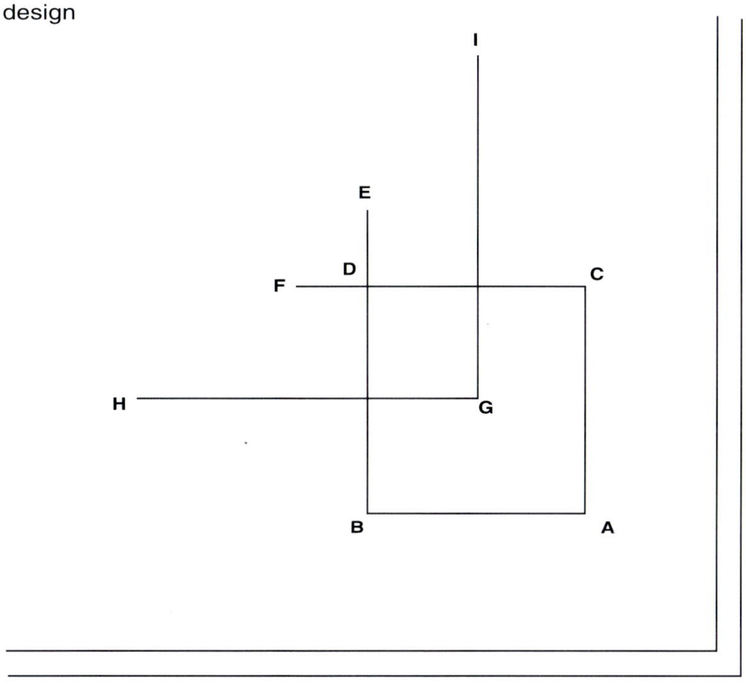

Starry sheet and pillowcase

Varying shades of yellow cotton give this embroidered moon impressive depth. The body is worked in long and short stitch and the eye in satin stitch.

Every child will love going to sleep with this sheet and pillowcase. Featuring a captivating moon and stars design with added sparkles of gold, it's bound to become a childhood favourite.

Finished size Sheet approximately 1.11 x 1.63 m; pillowcase 61 x 40 cm

Stitches

Long and short stitch
Satin stitch
Straight stitch

Materials

- 1.5 x 1.6 m cotton or polyester/cotton
- DMC stranded embroidery cotton: dark yellow (972), medium yellow (743), light yellow (726), very light yellow (727)
- Kreinik Balger blending filament in starry yellow
- Crewel embroidery needles mixed pack size 3/9
- 15 cm of 150 cm wide contrast fabric
- Matching thread
- Embroidery hoop
- Sharp lead pencil
- Scissors

SHEET

1 Cut a piece of cotton 1.5 m wide x 1.18 m long (see diagram on page 28). Fold over the side and bottom hems for 1 cm and press. Fold again for another 1 cm and press. Machine stitch all three hems.

2 Cut a length of contrast fabric 1.18 m x 8 cm. This will serve as the binding for the sheet. With right sides together, line the strip up to the raw edge of the sheet and pin, allowing 2 cm to extend beyond each side. Machine stitch 1 cm below the raw edge (see diagram on page 28).

3 Fold the binding back to reveal its right side and press. Fold in the ends and press, then fold down the top of the binding for 1 cm and press.

4 Fold 2.5 cm of the binding down so that approximately 1.5 cm is covering the raw edge of the sheet. Machine stitch in place, making sure the stitching runs along just below the binding on the opposite side of the sheet. You are now ready to work the embroidery (see page 29).

PILLOWCASE

1 Cut a piece of cotton 1.5 m x 42 cm. Fold both of its ends under 5 mm and press, then another 5 mm, press and machine. Fold one of these ends in for 20 cm and press.

2 Cut a strip of contrast fabric 3 x 4.5 cm. Fold the strip in half lengthwise, right side outside, and press. Place the raw edge of the strip inside the fold, lining it up against the crease line. Machine stitch the four layers, 1 cm from the fold for the length of the strip (see diagram on page 28).

3 Unfold the cotton fabric to reveal the contrasting trim. Fold the entire pillowcase in half with wrong sides facing and press the fold. Open out the pillowcase, trace the design onto the half with the trim and embroider as directed on page 29.

4 Fold each end for 10 cm onto the wrong side and press. Fold the pillowcase in half again, with right sides together, and machine down both sides, taking a

RIGHT Using long and short stitch and satin stitch, this matching bedroom set is quick and easy to make and will turn a child's bed into a canopy of dreams.

Sheet and pillowcase cutting guide

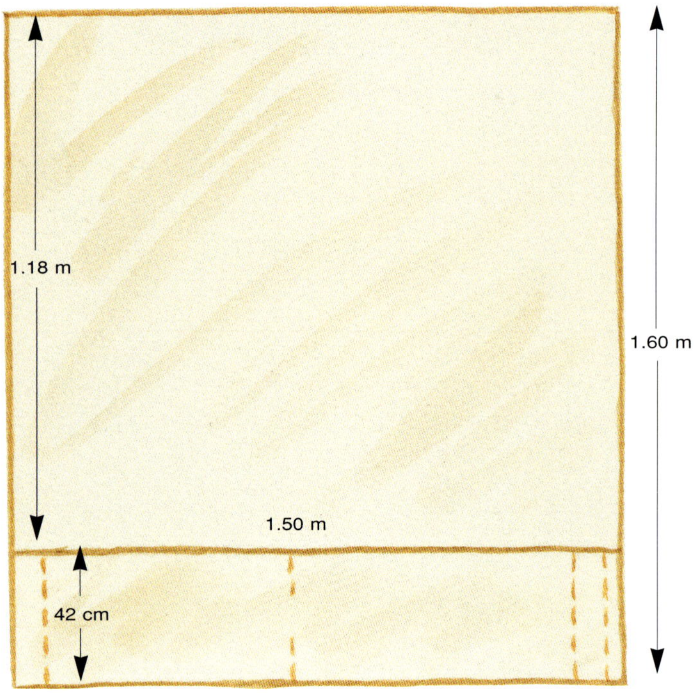

Binding sheet with contrast trim

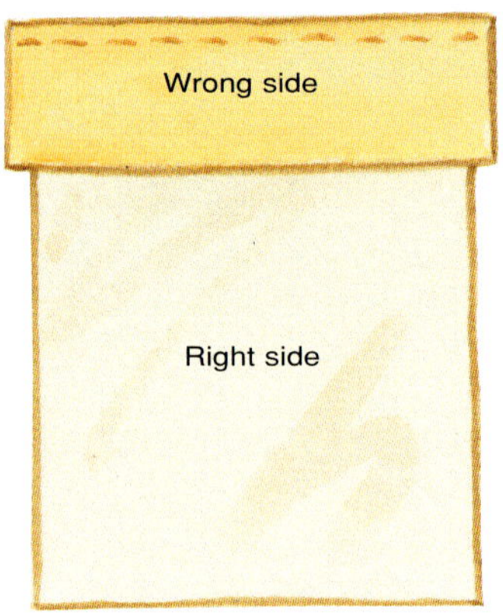

1 Machine stitch contrast fabric (binding) to top raw edge of sheet.

2 Fold binding back and press.

3 Fold in ends and top edge and press.

4 Fold 2.5 cm of binding down and machine stitch.

Making pillowcase with contrast trim

1 Fold top end in for 20 cm, place binding inside the fold and machine stitch.

2 Unfold cotton fabric to reveal trim.

3 After embroidering, fold each end in 10 cm and press.

4 Fold pillowcase in half with right sides together, bring the bottom flap over the top one, and machine stitch down both sides.

Moon and stars motif

1 cm seam allowance. Turn the pillowcase through to its right side and press.

EMBROIDERY

1 Using a sharp pencil, trace the design onto the cotton fabric by taping the design to a window, then placing the fabric on top. For the sheet, use the moon, two large stars and four small stars arranged as desired. Place the design near the binding. For the pillowcase, use the moon and three small stars and place the design near the corner of the folded end.

2 Work the embroidery as follows:

Moon. Use long and short stitch to work the moon, and satin stitch to work the eye. Work the moon's back in two strands of dark yellow (972) cotton and its front in medium yellow (743). Use very light yellow (727) for the eye, then work over it with one strand of blending filament.

Large stars. Use satin stitch and work each point in a different direction. Alternate between the light yellow (726) and the very light yellow (727) cottons. Work one strand of blending filament over each of the lighter points.

Small stars. Work these in the same way as the large stars but use medium yellow (743) and very light yellow (727) as the alternating colours. Work straight stitches in the centre using very light yellow (727) and then one strand of blending filament.

3 When the embroidery is finished, press on the wrong side.

USING STRANDED COTTON

- To enhance the embroidery's colour and texture, stranded cotton should always be 'stripped'—that is, you should separate the strands and then put them together again before beginning to stitch.
- When threading the needle, always thread the strands from the same ends, such as the cut ends. This makes the strands sit flatter and look neater on the fabric.
- It is best not to use lengths of cotton longer than 50 cm. A longer strand will rub against the fabric and eventually become worn, whereas a shorter strand will keep its fresh look.

A strand of gold blending filament is worked over each of the lighter points of the large star for extra sparkle.

Embroidered bookmarks

No avid reader ever has too many bookmarks. Drawing on the rich, bright colours of summer, these will bring a smile to your face whenever you open your book.

These assorted bookmarks are not only attractive pieces of embroidery, they are also very practical and make great gifts. Edged with nun's stitch and neat fringes, they are also a good introduction to Assisi and Hardanger embroidery techniques.

ASSISI TREES

Finished size 17 x 5 cm (without fringe)

Stitches

Cross stitch
Holbein stitch
Nun's stitch

Materials

- 25 x 10 cm of antique white evenweave linen with 12 threads to 1 cm
- DMC stranded embroidery cotton: orange (608), red copper (918)
- Tapestry needle size 26
- Ginnie Thompson 50/2 white linen thread
- Scissors

EMBROIDERY

1 Overcast the edges of the linen and mark the centre lines both vertically and horizontally with running stitch.

2 All stitches are worked over two threads each way on the linen. Referring to the chart, begin by embroidering the solid background of the design, using two strands of orange (608) cotton and working in cross stitch.

3 Work the outlines of each motif in holbein stitch using one strand of cotton: orange (608) for the double outer outline and red copper (918) for the outlines of the trees.

TO FINISH

1 To edge the bookmark, work a frame in nun's stitch using one strand of linen thread.

2 When completed, cut away the fabric close to the stitches on the long sides of the frame, and about 3 cm from the stitches on the short sides.

3 To form the fringes, withdraw the horizontal threads from the 3 cm of linen remaining at the top and bottom.

Assisi trees

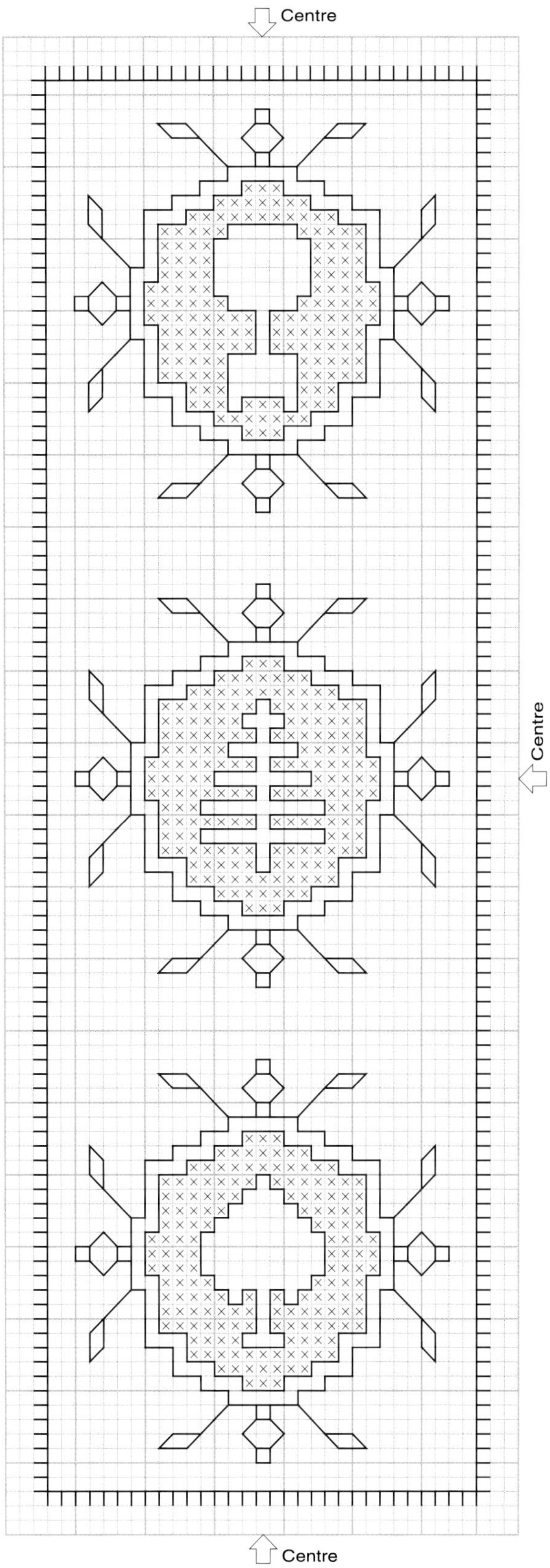

1 square = 2 linen threads

GREEN SAMPLER

Finished size 17 x 5 cm (without fringe)

Stitches

Cross stitch
Double back stitch
Holbein stitch
Nun's stitch
Smyrna cross stitch
Straight stitch
Wheat stitch

Materials

- 25 x 10 cm of antique white evenweave linen with 12 threads to 1 cm
- DMC stranded embroidery cotton: light emerald green (912), medium emerald green (911), dark emerald green (910), nile green (913)
- Tapestry needle size 26
- Ginnie Thompson 50/2 white linen thread
- Scissors

METHOD

1 Overcast the edges of the linen and mark the centre lines both vertically and horizontally with running stitch.

2 Work the embroidery as described below, referring to the chart:

Frame (A). Work in cross stitch using two strands of dark emerald green (910) cotton.

Light flowers (B). Work the centre in smyrna cross stitch and the petals in straight stitch, using two strands of light emerald green (912) cotton.

Small stars (C). Work in smyrna cross stitch, using two strands of nile green (913) cotton.

Zigzag lines (D). Work in holbein stitch, using two strands of medium emerald green (911) cotton.

Dark flowers (E). Work the centre in smyrna cross stitch and the petals in straight stitch, using two strands of medium emerald green (911) cotton.

Double lines (F). Work the double lines in double back stitch, using two strands of dark emerald green (910) cotton.

Sheaves (G). Work in wheat stitch, using two strands of light emerald green (912) cotton.

Beehive (H). Work in straight stitch, using one strand of nile green (913) cotton.

3 To finish, see 'Assisi trees'.

Green sampler

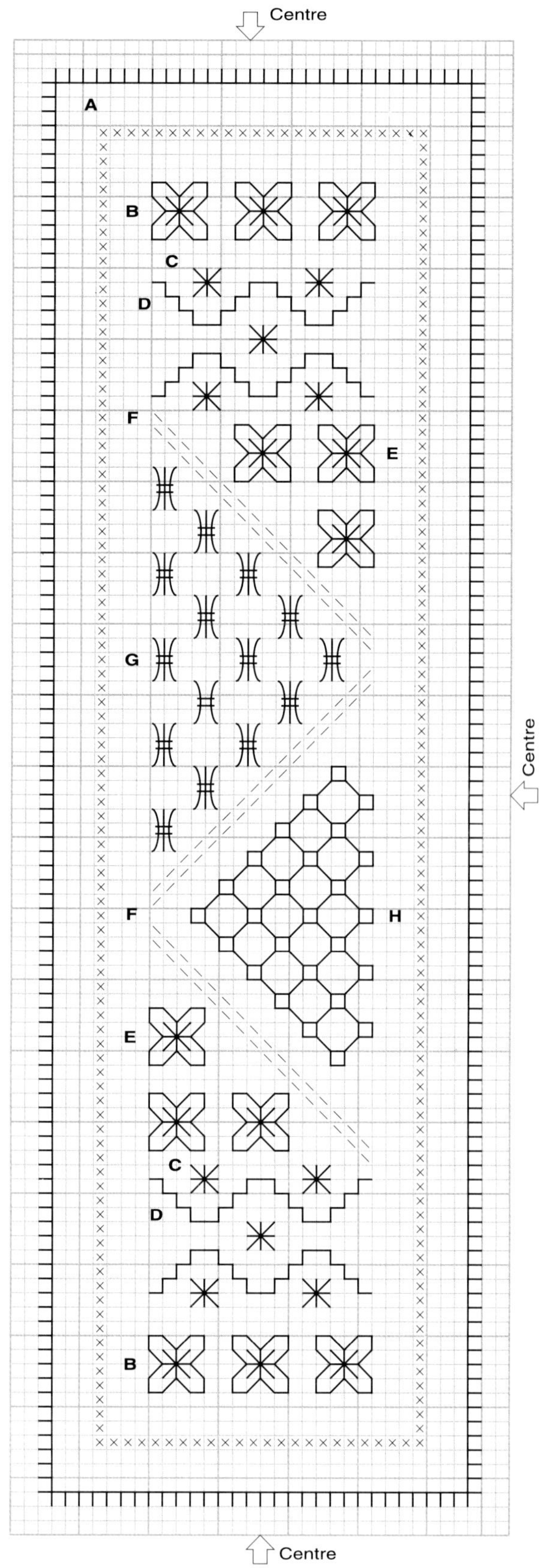

1 square = 2 linen threads

HARDANGER BOOKMARK

Finished size 17 x 5 cm (without fringe)

Stitches

Four-sided stitch
Needle weaving
Nun's stitch
Satin stitch
Spider web

Materials

- ◆ 25 x 10 cm of antique white evenweave linen with 12 threads to 1 cm
- ◆ DMC stranded embroidery cotton in yellow (973)
- ◆ Tapestry needle size 26
- ◆ Ginnie Thompson 50/2 white linen thread
- ◆ Embroidery hoop
- ◆ Small sharp embroidery scissors

METHOD

1 Overcast the edges of the linen and mark the centre lines both vertically and horizontally with running stitch.

2 Place the linen into the embroidery hoop. Before threading the needle, separate the strands of embroidery cotton and put them together again. Try to ensure that the strands lie beside each other without twisting.

3 Follow the chart for the embroidery, using two strands of cotton for the four-sided stitches and the kloster blocks. Kloster blocks are the basis of Hardanger embroidery and each block consists of five satin stitches worked over four threads. The blocks surround the cutwork area. See page 111.

4 All the kloster blocks must be worked before you begin cutting the fabric. Always cut on the back of the work, placing the scissors under the four threads with the scissor blade to the left of each kloster block. Cut only those threads that run between facing kloster blocks. Double check before you cut. Remove the threads carefully, leaving a grid of thread.

5 Begin needle weaving over the grid of threads, using two strands of cotton. Make a figure 8 under and over the weft threads, placing the needle under and over two threads at a time, and repeat the process until the bar has been filled.

6 Use one strand of cotton to work the spider webs.

7 To finish, see 'Assisi trees'.

Hardanger bookmark

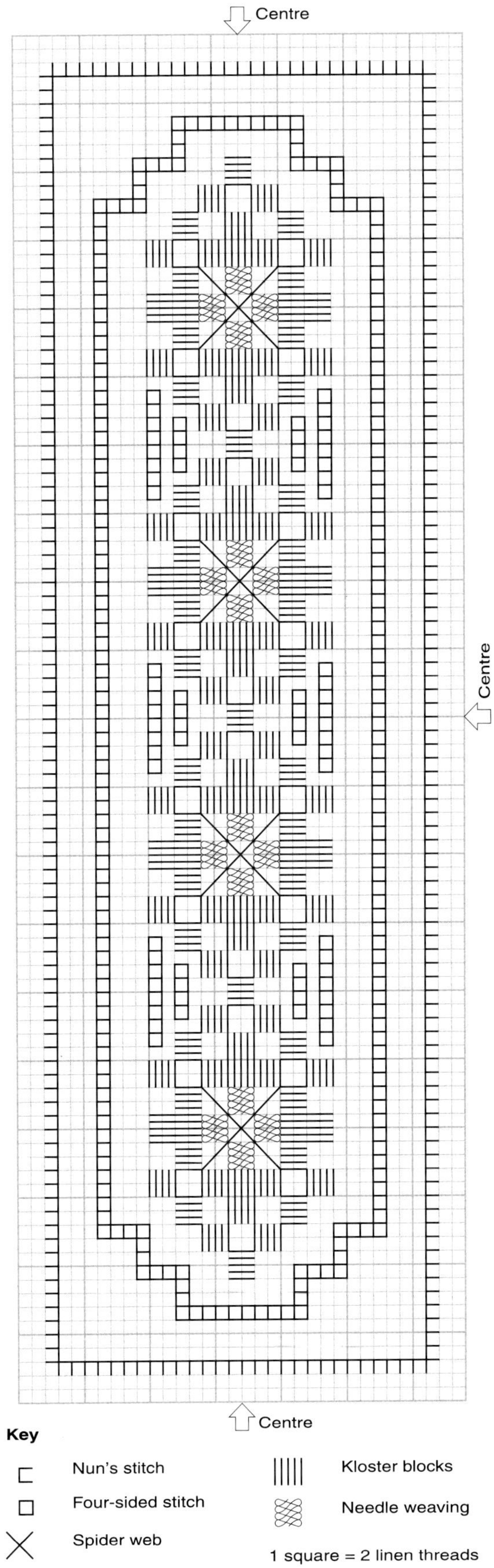

Chatelaine sewing set

The pin cushion, in the form of a little hat, sports multi-coloured embroidery on its underside, featuring flowers and buds.

This delightful chatelaine sewing set is made up of five storage items for all your sewing needs. It features bright floral motifs in padded satin stitch.

Finished size Hangs approximately 60 cm long

Stitches

Buttonhole stitch eyelet
Chain stitch
Colonial knot
Running stitch
Satin stitch
Stem stitch
Straight stitch

Materials

- 25 cm of plain fabric
- 25 cm of printed fabric
- DMC stranded embroidery cotton: deep yellow (972), pale yellow (744), red (666), yellow-green (3348), hunter green (3346), baby blue (334), medium pink (602), light pink (605), violet (3746)
- Crewel needle size 9
- 60–70 cm length of cord
- Embroidery hoop
- Quilter's thread to match plain fabric
- Two small, shanked buttons
- Two 14 x 10 cm pieces of felt
- Six macramé beads with holes large enough to thread cord
- One sheet of medium thickness cardboard
- Piece of thin cardboard (such as carton from a breakfast cereal)
- 3 cm wide section of a toilet or lunch paper roll.
- Piece of stiff paper
- Tape, ribbon or braid
- Piping to match plain fabric (optional)
- Pinking shears (optional)
- PVA adhesive
- Polyester filling
- Quilter's pencil (white or yellow) or iron-on transfer pencil and greaseproof paper

PREPARATION

Before you begin the embroidery, trace the outline of each item onto a piece of paper and cut them out to use as templates. Cut the following pieces from medium thickness cardboard:

Needle case: Four rectangles (see page 36).
Pin cushion: Four circles (see page 37).
Scissors sheath: Two backs and one front (see page 38).
Tape measure case: Four circles (see page 39) and two 14 x 3 cm strips (make sure the strips are cut along the grain as this will make bending them easier).
Thimble pip: from the thinner cardboard, cut six pieces (see page 37).

EMBROIDERY

1 Trace the motifs and outlines onto the plain fabric, leaving enough space between each to allow for seam allowances. You can do this freehand using a quilter's pencil or, if your material is not too dark, using an iron-on transfer pencil and greaseproof paper. The quilter's pencil rubs off easily so only do one piece at a time and work around each shape with one strand of the relevant coloured cotton in running stitch.

RIGHT Whether it's hung around your neck or on a hook, this set will keep all your essential sewing tools in perfect order.

147
148
149
150

2 For best results, use an embroidery hoop and work with two strands of cotton. Work the infill embroidery first in chain stitch to serve as padding, then work over this in satin stitch. Work the outlines and stems in stem stitch and the circular motifs in buttonhole stitch eyelets. Use straight stitches and colonial knots for the stamens.

3 Press the finished embroidery on the wrong side. Cut out each piece, allowing 1 cm seam allowances.

NEEDLE CASE

1 Take the embroidered rectangle and cut a rectangle the same size from the printed fabric. Place the embroidered rectangle on top of the printed one, right sides together, and machine stitch down the right-hand side, 1 cm from the edge. Trim the seam to 5 mm and press flat.

2 Take two of the cardboard rectangles and place them on the wrong side of this piece, 5 mm apart (to allow for the thickness of the felt pages). Place adhesive across the top and bottom of the cardboard pieces and glue them in place. Glue the seam allowance down, then glue down each end, trimming the corners free of bulk.

3 Cut one 18 x 12.5 cm piece of printed fabric, place the remaining two cardboard pieces on the wrong side, 5 mm apart, and repeat the gluing process.

4 Glue both sections together. Using the crewel needle and a length of quilter's thread doubled, work around all four edges stitching the two thicknesses together with small stitches as shown in the diagram.

Stitching around the edges

5 Take the two pieces of felt and, if desired, trim them with pinking shears. Centre them over the centre seam and ensure they fit neatly inside the book. From the outside, machine stitch neatly down the seam between the plain and printed fabric, making sure the felt pages are kept straight.

6 Stitch a small button to the back and work a buttonhole stitch loop on the front of the case. Work another buttonhole loop on the top left-hand corner of the book, between the front and back covers. This is for threading onto the cord later.

Needle case

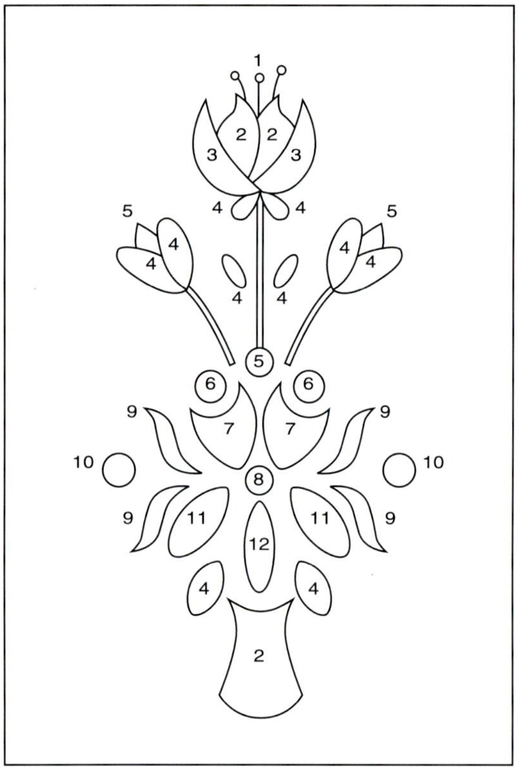

DMC colour key

Filler colour given first, followed by outline colour.

- **1** 666 Red
- **2** 3746 Violet; 972 Deep yellow
- **3** 605 Light pink; 602 Medium pink
- **4** 3348 Yellow-green; 3346 Hunter green
- **5** 666 Red; 972 Deep yellow
- **6** 334 Baby blue; 3746 Violet
- **7** 602 Medium pink; 605 Light pink
- **8** 3746 Violet; 666 Red
- **9** 744 Pale yellow; 972 Deep yellow
- **10** 3746 Violet
- **11** 334 Baby blue; 602 Medium pink
- **12** 605 Light pink; 972 Deep yellow

All stems in hunter green 3346

THIMBLE PIP

1 Cut five pieces from the printed fabric, adding a 1 cm seam allowance.

2 Starting at one of the pointed ends, work small running stitches around the top edge of each fabric piece, 5 mm from the edge. Finish at the opposite pointed end, then start from this end to work around the bottom edge. Repeat the process for the embroidered piece.

3 Place a cardboard piece on the wrong side of each fabric piece and pull the stitching up to cover the cardboard. Tie a knot at each end.

4 Glue the pieces in pairs so that you have two pairs of printed pieces and one pair of plain embroidered and printed fabric.

Thimble pip

DMC colour key

Filler colour given first, followed by outline colour.

1	744 Pale yellow
2	972 Deep yellow
3	3746 Violet; 605 Light pink
4	602 Medium pink; 666 Red
5	334 Baby blue
6	3346 Hunter green
7	3348 Yellow-green; 3346 Hunter green

All stems in hunter green 3346

5 Using quilter's thread doubled, stitch one edge of the embroidered section, catching together the outer edge and the inner edge with small stitches as with the needle case. Do the same with one side of another piece (these will be the opening edges of the pip).

6 Stitch the three sections together leaving the finished edges open from point to point. Take care not to crush the cardboard. The pip opens when its corners are gently squeezed. Work a buttonhole loop at one point of the pip.

PIN CUSHION

1 Take the embroidered circle and cut a circle the same size from the printed fabric. Using small running stitches work around each circle, stitching within the seam allowance.

2 Place a cardboard circle on the wrong side of each fabric circle and gently pull the stitches up so that the fabric gathers around the cardboard. Tie the ends and glue both pieces together. Using quilter's thread doubled, neaten the edge in the same way as for the previous two pieces.

3 Cut a 14 cm diameter circle from the printed fabric and work running stitches around its edge. Take the 3 cm wide section of a toilet or lunch paper roll, fill it with polyester filling and place it in the centre of the fabric circle. Pull up the gathers and tie off.

4 Apply adhesive to the edge on the bottom of the roll and glue it down carefully to the centre of the

Pin cushion

DMC colour key

Filler colour given first, followed by outline colour.

1	3746 Violet; 334 Baby blue
2	605 Light pink; 602 Medium pink
3	3348 Yellow-green; 3346 Hunter green
4	3346 Hunter green
5	334 Baby blue
6	972 Deep yellow
7	744 Pale yellow
8	744 Pale yellow; 666 Red
9	3746 Violet; 605 Light pink

All stems in hunter green 3346

large printed circle. Stitch it into position with small invisible stitches.

5 Trim the hat as desired by applying braid, ribbon or even small plastic flowers (as was done here). Work a buttonhole loop on the edge of the hat.

SCISSORS SHEATH

1 Cut two back pattern pieces from the printed fabric, adding a 1 cm seam allowance. Work running stitch around the fabric and cover two cardboard pieces in the same way as for the thimble pip. Glue these covered pieces together and stitch them with quilter's thread doubled along the top edge and 2 cm down each side.

2 Cover the front cardboard piece with the embroidered fabric in the same way and, if desired, add piping to the top edge and neaten off by gluing a piece of stiff paper to the back.

3 Stitch the front and back sections into position, catching the three thicknesses of the case together. Work a buttonhole loop in the centre top.

TAPE MEASURE CASE

1 Trim two of the cardboard circles and one of the strips down a fraction.

2 Cut three circles of printed fabric, adding a 1 cm seam allowance. Cover the four cardboard circles with the fabric ones (make sure you use a larger

Scissors sheath

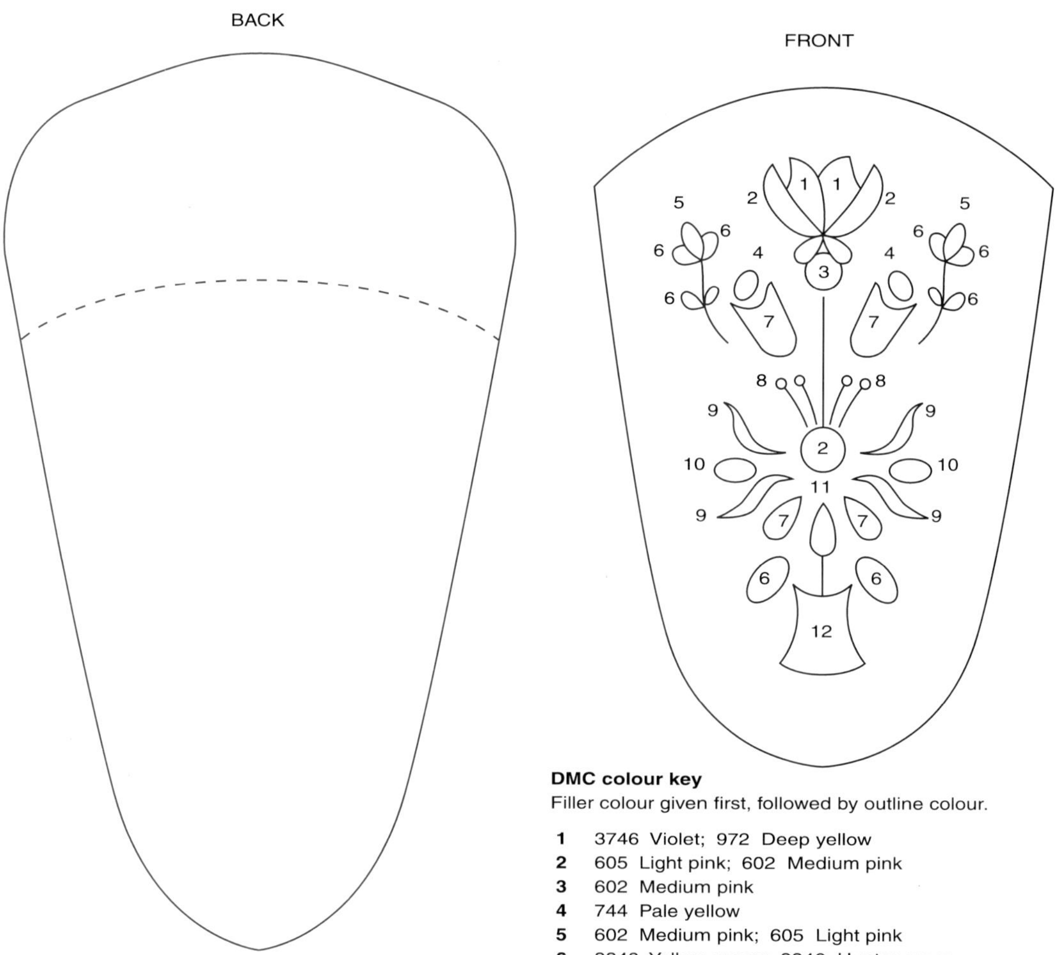

DMC colour key
Filler colour given first, followed by outline colour.

1 3746 Violet; 972 Deep yellow
2 605 Light pink; 602 Medium pink
3 602 Medium pink
4 744 Pale yellow
5 602 Medium pink; 605 Light pink
6 3348 Yellow-green; 3346 Hunter green
7 334 Baby blue; 602 Medium pink
8 666 Red
9 744 Pale yellow; 972 Deep yellow
10 3746 Violet; 602 Medium pink
11 744 Pale yellow; 3746 Violet
12 602 Medium pink; 666 Red
All stems in hunter green 3346

circle for the embroidered piece) in the same way as for the pin cushion. Glue the smaller circles to the bigger circles.

3 Cut two 14 x 3 cm strips from the printed fabric, adding a 1 cm seam allowance, and glue down to each cardboard strip, trimming the corners to avoid unsightly bulk.

4 Glue the two strips wrong sides together. Place the glued strips between the two circles, allowing the strip to overlap to form a flap, and stitch together with quilter's thread doubled. Leave approximately 5 cm open. Finish the open edges stitching through the two circle thicknesses.

5 Work a buttonhole loop on the end of the overlapping strip (flap) and add a button for fastening. Work a buttonhole loop approximately 10 cm down from the button.

TO FINISH

1 Thread one of the items onto the cord and tie a knot on either side of the item approximately 15–20 cm apart.

2 Thread a macramé bead onto each of these knots, then tie another knot at the end of each bead. The beads should be firmly held in place by the knots and serve to keep the items neatly separated.

3 Continue threading the other items and beads, making further knots 15–20 cm apart so that, when hanging, each item rests neatly on top of a knot and bead. Tie the ends in a bow and hang.

A simpler motif is worked on the tape measure case, but the same colours are used for continuity.

Tape measure case

DMC colour key

Filler colour given first, followed by outline colour.

1	3348 Yellow-green; 3346 Hunter green
2	605 Light pink; 3746 Violet
3	602 Medium pink; 666 Red
4	744 Pale yellow; 972 Deep yellow
5	972 Deep yellow; 3346 Hunter green
6	605 Light pink; 602 Medium pink
7	3746 Violet
8	666 Red

All stems in hunter green 3346

WORKING IN SATIN STITCH

- To make satin stitch look its very best, it is essential to keep an even tension when working the embroidery so as to not distort the fabric.
- Always use an embroidery hoop and work each stitch in two moves—up and down in a stabbing motion—rather than one.
- Always strip the stranded cotton before you begin working the embroidery (see page 29).
- To ensure you get a full and even coverage, it is a good idea to continue stripping the stranded cotton as you work. To do this, slide the needle down the thread onto the fabric and separate the strands. Then take the needle back up the thread and resume stitching.
- Although it is not essential, satin stitch always looks best when it is stitched over chain stitch.
- When filling in a curved shape, make the first stitch at the centre of the shape, ensuring that it is at right angles to it. Work outwardly, then return the needle to the centre and continue stitching toward the other corner.

Seashell hand towels

Variegated cotton in terracotta and gold-brown makes these embroidered seashells come to life.

The crisp feel of linen, the charm of embroidered seashells and the daintiness of a hem stitched hem make these hand towels an absolute luxury. They are the perfect welcome to a special guest.

Finished size 30 x 45 cm

Stitches

Buttonhole stitch
Fly stitch
Ladder hem stitch
Stem stitch

Materials

- Two 32.5 x 50 cm pieces of Belfast linen
- DMC variegated stranded cotton: terracotta (69), gold-brown (61)
- Tapestry needle size 26
- Crewel needle size 9
- Quilting thread to match linen
- Dressmaker's carbon
- Pencil and scissors

METHOD

1 Cut the fabric carefully along the grain of the weave. Machine narrow hems along the long sides.
2 Measure 4.5 cm from the short sides and cut three horizontal threads in the middle. Carefully withdraw each thread up to the side hems and cut, leaving enough length to thread a needle and weave into the side hems before cutting off completely.
3 Turn a hem into each lower edge of the drawn threads and baste. Work ladder hem stitch with the quilting thread and tapestry needle, catching in two vertical linen threads and the hem turning. Hem stitch the upper row, catching in the corresponding two threads as for the lower row.
4 Trace the shell designs and transfer them to the linen using dressmaker's carbon or your preferred method. It is advisable to transfer one shell at a time as the design may fade with handling.
5 Use gold-brown (61) cotton for one hand towel and terracotta (69) for the other. Cut the variegated cotton to give the most pleasing colour effect, discarding some if there seems too much of either dark or light tones. Separate two strands of cotton, then realign them before threading the crewel needle, so that they will not twist together. Work the design as shown, using buttonhole, stem and fly stitches.

Seashell designs

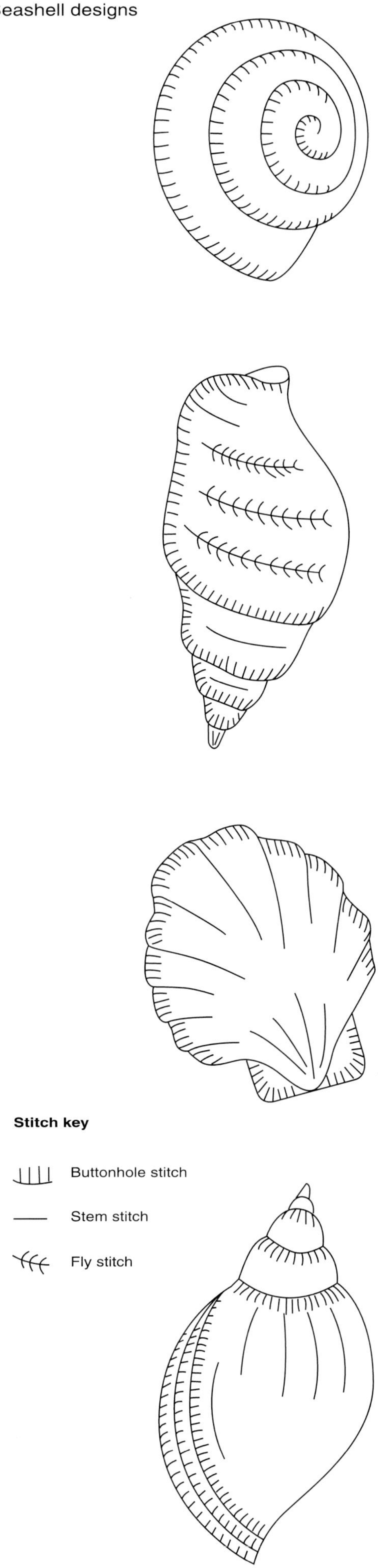

Shadow work greeting cards

Your family and friends will be delighted to receive a shadow work greeting card. Here are three floral designs to choose from, each sporting a primary colour offset by the lovely cream background.

Finished size 15 x 10.5 cm

Stitches

Double back stitch (shadow stitch)

Materials

- Three cards with cut-out windows
- DMC stranded embroidery cotton: orange-red (606), apricot (3340), avocado green (472), fern green (522), green-grey (3052), bright canary (973), deep canary (972), royal blue (796), delft (798)
- 20 cm square of cream cotton batiste for each card
- Quilting needle size 10
- Embroidery hoop
- Double-sided tape
- Pencil
- Spray adhesive

Convolvulus motif

DMC colour key

Flower petals in delft (798)
Flower base in royal blue (796)
Leaves and stems in green-grey (3052)

X Suggested starting point

This shadow work is embroidered from the right side of the fabric using stranded embroidery cotton.

EMBROIDERY

1 Place the fabric in the embroidery hoop, then place the hoop upside down onto the design.

2 Trace the design with a pencil. Remove the fabric from the hoop and reposition it so that the design is now on top, ready to be worked.

3 Work the embroidery. Work the shadow work from the right side of the fabric in double back stitch, with one strand of cotton in the quilting needle. Always start with a waste knot which will be fastened off later. Embroider the flower petals in numerical order—many of the petals have a common edge, so it is important to embroider them in the correct sequence. Bring the needle to the front of the fabric, 2 mm from the tip of a petal shape or at a suggested starting point, as marked on each design. Make a small back stitch, take the thread across the back of the design and make a small back stitch on the opposite side. Then return the needle back to the starting point.

RIGHT A homemade gift is always much more special than one bought at a shop. Use these for birthdays, anniversaries or just to show you care.

4 Continue working the embroidery making small, even back stitches. On the curves adjust the stitches: smaller ones on the inside curve, larger ones on the outside curve.

5 Where the design shares a common line, pick up the threads at the back of the work. After making a stitch through the fabric from front to back, put the needle around a finished stitch in order to bring the thread back to the front again. It should give a herringbone effect on the back of the fabric. Finish each thread on the wrong side as close as possible to the edge.

6 When the embroidery is completed, wash it with a mild soap in warm water and rinse well. When slightly damp, iron it.

MAKING UP THE CARD

1 Trim the embroidered square so it fits neatly inside the card.

2 With the card wrong side up, place the embroidery's wrong side on the left flap and fold the flap over so that the embroidery can now be seen through the cut-out window of the card. This is your chance to ensure that you have positioned the embroidery accurately.

3 Once you are sure the embroidery is positioned correctly, mark lightly with a pencil around it so you can later return the embroidery to the correct place for gluing.

4 Remove the embroidery and ensure there are no loose strands of cotton anywhere on the wrong side of the work.

5 Spray adhesive lightly on the left flap of the card, keeping a piece of scrap paper over the rest of the card to protect it.

6 Position the embroidery on the card and firmly press down.

7 Take the double-sided tape and place it around the cut-out window of the card, as well as around the edges of that centre section.

8 Press the centre section firmly over the embroidered flower.

Iris motif

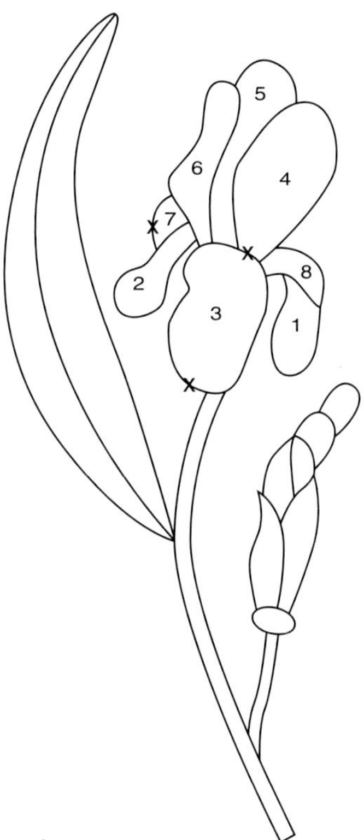

DMC colour key

Flower petals 1, 2 and 6 in deep canary (972)
Flower petals 3, 4, 5, 7 and 8 in bright canary (973)
Buds in deep canary (972)
Leaves and stems in fern green (522)
X Suggested starting point

Poppies motif

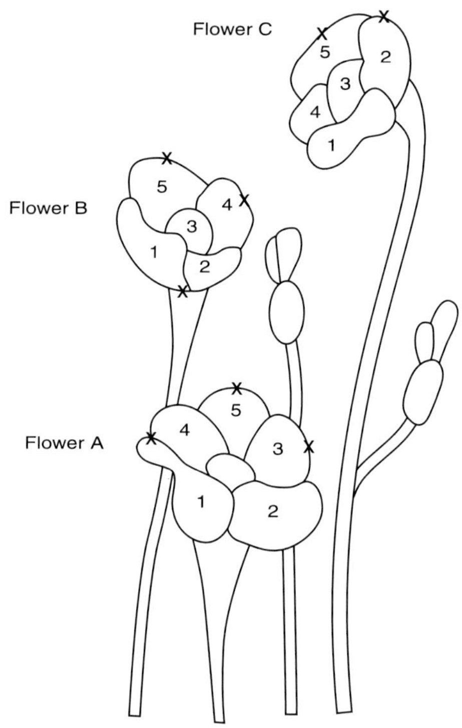

DMC colour key

Flower A in apricot (3440)
Flower B in orange-red (606)
Flower C in apricot (3440)
Buds in orange-red (606)
Stems and flower centres in avocado green (472)
X Suggested starting point

Double back stitch (also known as shadow stitch) is the only stitch used on these impressive greeting cards.

As the colour of the cotton shows through the fabric, it creates an almost three-dimensional effect.

CARING FOR YOUR EMBROIDERY

When you've put so much hard work into a project like your embroidery, you want it to last a long time. The way in which you use, wash and store your piece will largely determine its lifespan.

The first and best step is always prevention. To protect your embroidery from quick deterioration, follow these guidelines:

- Use good quality threads and fabrics that will last longer and give better results.
- Keep your work as clean as possible. Always wash your hands before working on or handling your embroidery, and keep any work-in-progress folded away neatly in a bag or box.
- When you stop stitching, remove the hoop so that it won't mark your work.
- Never leave the needle inserted in the fabric or it may leave rust marks.
- Generally, you should not expose your embroidery to temperatures above 17° C. Strong sunlight, very bright lights and heat can fade colours and weaken the threads.
- Keep your unfinished embroidery in a dark, dry place, away from damp.

If you find it necessary to wash your embroidered piece, keep the following in mind.

- Before washing, test the embroidery to check that it is colourfast.
- Always wash each piece of embroidery separately and by hand.
- Use a mild soap in warm water.
- After rinsing, roll the embroidery between two clean towels and squeeze gently but do not wring. Unroll the towels and spread the embroidery out flat to dry on a towel.
- If the fabric is not washable, you can use a stain remover to remove marks but test it first on a scrap of the fabric.

Embroidery should never be dry cleaned as it may cause a chemical reaction with the thread dyes. If dry cleaning is essential, however, be sure to explain this to the dry cleaner.

Always iron an embroidered piece on its wrong side with a clean cloth over it. If the piece is dry, use a damp cloth. Press with a warm steam iron, and avoid any ironing preparations or protectors as they may interfere with thread dyes.

Ribbon floral pictures

The luxury of pure silk ribbon is used here to create three gorgeous floral pictures featuring cosmos, lilacs, roses, hollyhock and daisies.

Large stem stitch is used to work this golden basket.

Finished size of embroidery Flowers in a basket 7.5 cm high x 10 cm wide; flowers in a bowl 9 cm high x 9 cm wide; flowers in a garden 9 cm high x 11 cm wide

Stitches

Blanket stitch
Chain stitch
Detached chain stitch
Fly stitch
French knot
Short stitch
Stem stitch
Straight stitch

Materials

- Three 25 cm squares of homespun
- 15 cm (6 in) embroidery hoop
- 7 mm wide pure silk ribbon in dark red, medium mauve and yellow
- 4 mm wide pure silk ribbon in dark lilac, gold, pale gold, dark blue-green, medium yellow-green and burgundy
- 2 mm wide pure silk ribbon in dark red, burgundy, dark blue-green, medium mauve and yellow-green
- Chenille needles sizes 18, 20, 24
- Crewel needles sizes 8, 9, 10
- Rajmahal art silk in light green (3551)
- Madeira Decora embroidery rayon: gold (1571), pale gold (1470)
- Lola rayon twisted thread in dark green (167)
- DMC stranded embroidery cotton: blue-green (501), golden brown (975)
- Novelty buttons: 1 bird house (or similar), 1 girl (or boy), 1 dog (or cat or bird), 2 small red beetles, 1 pair gold scissors, 8 faux pearl buttons
- Six small red buttons

LEFT The depth of rich burgundy and purple is cleverly offset by the touches of gold throughout these pictures.

- Burgundy beads
- Yellow beads
- H pencil
- Scissors

EMBROIDERY

■ Silk ribbon is fragile so use only short lengths of about 25–30 cm. Thread the ribbon through the eye of the needle, pull it through past the tip, hold the tip of the needle and pull the long end of the ribbon through to secure it (see the diagram on page 6).

■ Leave a tail of about 8 mm behind your work and stitch it down as you work. Leave a tail behind your work when finished and secure with a stitch.

■ Use chenille needle size 18 for the 7 mm ribbon, size 20 for the 4 mm ribbon and size 24 for the 2 mm ribbon. Use a size 8 crewel needle for the Lola rayon and the Madeira rayon in pale gold (1470), and a size 9 crewel needle for the Decora rayon in gold (1571). Use either a size 9 or 10 crewel needle for the stranded embroidery cotton and art silk.

■ Work the flowers as follows:

Cosmos. Using 7 mm medium mauve ribbon, work five evenly spaced 1 cm long petals, folding the ribbon over with a ribbon stitch. Work a French knot loosely in the centre with 4 mm burgundy ribbon and surround it with burgundy beads. The stems and leaves are worked in stem stitch with two strands of light green (3551) art silk. Curve the stems gently and work a small detached chain stitch at the top of each one.

Lilacs. Work French knots to form a cone about 1.5 cm long, with 4 mm dark lilac ribbon. Use one strand of dark green (167) Lola rayon to work the stems in stem stitch and the leaves in detached chain stitch.

Large roses. Use 7 mm dark red ribbon and make a five-legged evenly spaced frame to weave the ribbon through, a little smaller than the size of the spider's web rose. Bring the needle up at the centre and weave the ribbon over and under the frame until it's the size you desire. Take the ribbon to the back of the work and leave a 'tail' to stitch down. Buds are a short detached chain stitch worked in the same ribbon, with the calyx being a short stitch on each side worked in 4 mm dark blue-green ribbon. The leaves are three short straight stitches, also worked in 4 mm dark

Rose frame

blue-green ribbon. Work the stems in two strands of blue-green (501) cotton in stem stitch.

Small roses. Work as for the large roses but start with a smaller frame and use 2 mm dark red ribbon. The leaves are smaller straight stitches worked with 2 mm dark blue-green ribbon.

Hollyhock. Cut 10 cm of yellow 7 mm silk ribbon. Join into a circle and work running stitches along the inside edge. Gather tightly and stitch onto the fabric. Stitch a small red button in the centre and a yellow bead on top.The leaves are worked in detached chain stitch using 4 mm medium yellow-green ribbon.

Daisies. As with the cosmos, work five small evenly spaced petals, folding the ribbon over with a ribbon stitch. For the daisies in the garden, use 4 mm gold silk ribbon, make the petals 4 mm long and work a straight stitch over each petal from the centre of the flower with two strands of gold (1571) Decora rayon.

Novelty buttons are incorporated into this pretty garden to add a unique touch.

The daisies in the basket are worked the same way but should have 5 mm long petals with two stitches worked over each one. The daisies in the bowl are worked in 4 mm pale gold ribbon, have 6 mm petals and three stitches over each one. Stitch a burgundy bead in the centre of each daisy. All the daisies have foliage of one strand of dark green (167) Lola rayon worked in fly stitch.

Asters. With 2 mm medium mauve ribbon, work a small circle of straight stitches, from the centre to the outside. Keep going around about three times, until the flower is raised. With 2 mm burgundy ribbon, work a French knot in the centre. Work the stems in stem stitch using two strands of light green (3551) art silk, and add a detached chain stitch at the top of some.

Tulips. Use 7 mm yellow ribbon to work a long detached chain stitch in the centre and a slightly shorter one on either side. Work a few straight stitches for the stems and leaves, using 2 mm yellow-green ribbon.

FLOWERS IN A BASKET

1 With the pencil, trace the outline of the basket onto a square of homespun and mark the position of the flowers and buttons.

2 Embroider the basket first, using four strands of pale gold (1470) Decora embroidery rayon. Work the basket in large stem stitch and the handle in chain stitch.

3 Embroider the flowers, then the leaves and stems. Attach the scissors and beetles where they belong.

FLOWERS IN A BOWL

1 Trace the outline of the bowl onto a square of homespun and mark the position of the flowers (see the design on page 50).

2 Embroider the outline (including the top) and base of the bowl in stem stitch, using two strands of gold (1571) Decora embroidery rayon. Starting at the top, fill the bowl in with rows of blanket stitch, starting each alternate row so that you are stitching into the spaces above. Embroider the flowers.

FLOWERS IN A GARDEN

1 Place the homespun square on top of the design (see page 50) and, using either a light box or a window, trace the picture onto the fabric. With the pencil, lightly mark the position of the flowers and buttons and the stems of the rose bush. Don't make the lines too heavy because they cannot be removed once the picture is embroidered. Also mark the position of the buttons.

2 Start at the top of the picture and work down. Embroider the flowers as directed, then add the leaves and stems. Stitch the faux pearl buttons on for the path, then add straight stitches around them with golden brown (975) cotton.

3 If any of the buttons have shanks at the back, make a mark where they will go on the wrong side of the fabric and make small buttonholes for the shanks to fit through. Stitch the buttons on, taking the thread across the buttonhole.

Flowers in a basket

Flowers in a bowl

Key

 Cosmos

 Lilac

 Hollyhock

 Large daisies

 Large roses

Flowers in a garden

Key

 Small roses

 Asters

 Tulips

 Lilac

 Small daisies

Tapestry travel set

Your make-up, jewellery or glasses will no longer float around the bottom of your bag when you make this attractive matching set of jewellery roll, make-up bag and glasses case. This project is recommended only for those with advanced sewing skills.

Finished size Jewellery roll 26 x 11 cm (before folding); make-up bag 24 x 6 x 12 cm; glasses case 22 x 11 cm

Stitches

Tent stitch

Materials

- 50 cm x 1 m of 14-count mono canvas
- Approximately 1 m of navy brocade
- Approximately 50 cm of navy polypoplin for lining
- DMC Laine Colbert tapestry wool: two large skeins and three small skeins of navy (7299), seven skeins of orange (7052), five skeins of blue (7314), nine skeins of green (7342), five skeins of white (1530), eight skeins of red (7606)
- Tapestry needle size 18
- Tapestry frame
- 4 m of navy cotton cord
- 50 cm of 1.5 cm wide navy grosgrain ribbon
- 30 cm of 1 cm wide navy twill weave cotton tape
- 25 cm of 2.5 cm wide navy twill weave cotton tape
- 25 cm navy zip
- 12 cm navy zip (oversew the bottom end of a larger zip and cut to size)
- Thin polyester wadding or pellon
- Two navy velcro dots
- Two small black press studs
- Navy machine thread
- Scissors and pencil

JEWELLERY ROLL

EMBROIDERY

1 Cut a piece of canvas 30 x 15 cm and work the tapestry in tent stitch (see chart on page 53).

2 When the tapestry is complete, you will need to block it. Steam the canvas lightly but do not allow the iron to touch the surface of the work. Pull gently into shape and trim the canvas to size, allowing a 1.5 cm seam allowance.

This attractive tapestry jewellery roll is worked entirely in tent stitch using tapestry wool on mono canvas.

THE LINING

Cut a 30 x 15 cm piece of polypoplin to use as the lining. With the long sides horizontal to you, pencil in a line from top to bottom to mark the vertical centre of the fabric.

THE TAPES

1 Cut two 10 cm strips of the 1 cm wide twill weave tape. Take the first strip and, folding under the raw edges, sew each end of the strip to the lining in the top right-hand corner, approximately 2 cm from the raw edges. Take the second strip and sew it on the same way, 1 cm below the first strip. Post earrings can be pushed through these tapes and the butterfly clips pushed onto the posts. See the diagram on page 53.

2 Take the 25 x 2.5 cm twill weave tape, fold it in half and sew down each long side leaving 2 cm open at the folded end. Stitch the folded end flat. Fill the tube with wadding leaving 2 cm free at the mouth. Baste this raw end to the vertical centre of the lining, approximately 2 cm below the other strips of tape. Stitch a velcro dot onto the other end of the tube and onto the fabric. Rings can be slipped onto this tube and held in place.

Earring tape

Ring tape

POCKET AND FLAP

1 Cut two pieces of polypoplin, 15.5 x 12 cm and 15.5. x 4.5 cm, and overlock all edges. Fold a long side of each piece down 1.5 cm and press. Take the 12 cm zip and position it parallel so that the nearest row of teeth sits against the folded edge of the larger piece. Ensure you leave at least 3 cm at each end of the zip. Pin the zip into place. Take the smaller piece of fabric and place it over the zip so that its folded edge meets the folded edge of the larger piece. Machine sew a rectangle all around the zip, stitching 2 mm from the folded edge of the larger piece and 1 cm from the folded edge of the smaller piece.

2 Place the fabric with the zip face down on the right side of the lining with its raw edge approximately 5 mm to the left of the centre mark. Machine stitch them together and turn the fabric with the zip back over to the left side. Hand baste around the three remaining edges to form a pocket.

3 Cut a piece of polypoplin 13.5 x 13 cm. Join the long edges right sides

LEFT *This practical matching travel set is ideal for frequent travellers.*

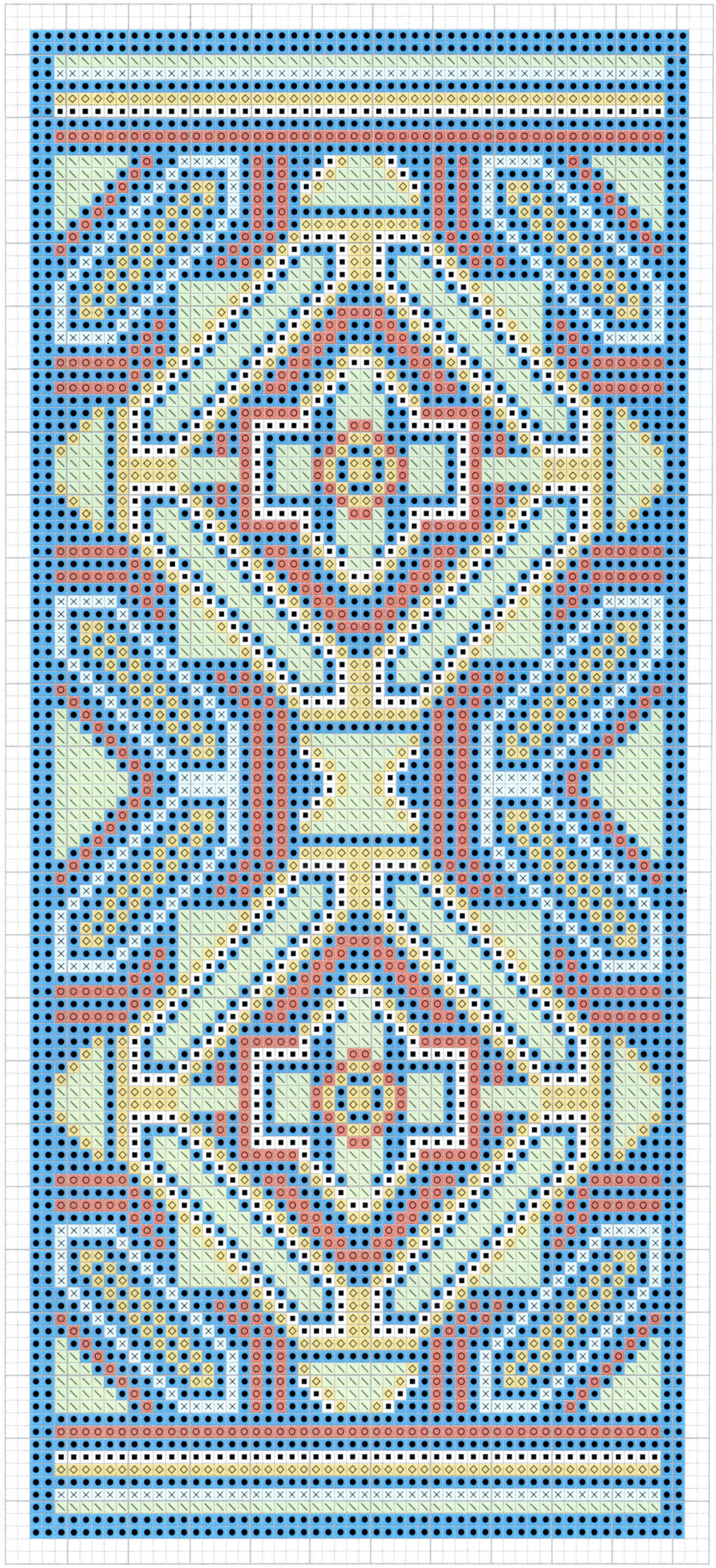

Jewellery roll

DMC colour key

■	7299	Navy
◇	7052	Orange
×	7314	Blue
\	7342	Green
▪	1530	White
○	7606	Red

The jewellery roll includes a zipped pocket, two earring posts (hidden by a flap, top right-hand corner) and a ring tube.

together and machine sew. Place the seam in the centre of the back and press. Machine sew one of the open ends and turn to the right side. This piece will serve as a flap over the earring tapes. Pin the flap into position over the tapes with the raw edge level with that of the right edge of the lining. Hand baste it into position and sew two press studs to the free corners.

TO FINISH

1 Cut two 25 cm strips of the grosgrain ribbon. Join one end of each grosgrain strip to the centre of a short side of the canvas and sew into place.

2 Take the lining, complete with zip, tapes and flap, and place it on the tapestry right sides together. Pin, baste and machine stitch around the edges leaving approximately 8 cm open on one side to turn through. Trim the seams to 7 mm and cut the bulk from the corners. Turn right side out.

3 Stitch the 8 cm slit closed invisibly by hand, leaving a 1 cm hole open.

4 Take the cord and tuck one end into the 1 cm hole. Sew the cord by hand along the seam and end by tucking the other end into the hole. Secure with a few small stitches. Fold the finished roll in half and tie closed with the grosgrain ribbons.

MAKE-UP BAG

EMBROIDERY

1 Cut a piece of canvas 26 x 16 cm and work the tapestry in tent stitch (see chart on page 55).

2 When the tapestry is complete, you will need to block it. Steam the canvas lightly but do not allow the iron to touch the surface of the work. Pull gently into shape and trim the canvas to size, allowing a 1.5 cm seam allowance and curving the corners gently.

MAKING UP THE BAG

1 Cut a piece of brocade, same size and shape as the worked canvas. This will form the back of the bag.

2 Cut two strips of brocade approximately 28 x 6 cm. For each piece, fold down one long side 1.5–2 cm and press. Take the 25 cm zip and position it beneath one of the fabric pieces so that a row of teeth sits against the folded edge. Pin the zip into place. Take the second piece of fabric and place it over the zip so that its folded edge meets the folded edge of the first piece. Machine sew a rectangle all around the zip, stitching 2 mm from the folded edge of the first piece of fabric and 1 cm from the folded edge of the second piece of fabric. The finished strip with the zipper in place should be 9 cm wide.

3 Cut a strip of brocade 9 cm wide and approximately 44 cm long for the gusset (measure around your tapestry to obtain the exact measurement and add a seam allowance to each end).

4 Cut 10 cm of 1 cm twill weave tape. Fold in half and sew to the right side of one end of the 9 x 44 cm brocade, about 1.5–2 cm from the raw edge. This will be the tab for holding the bag when the zip is closed.

5 Place the wrong sides of both 9 cm wide pieces of brocade together and machine sew at the ends, ensuring that the tab meets the bottom end of the zip. Turn through to the right side.

6 Open the zipper. With right sides together, pin and machine stitch the gusset to the brocade back and tapestry front of the bag. The zip should be positioned across the top.

TO FINISH

1 Make a bag the same size from polypoplin in the same way (but without the zip or the tab). Place the lining inside the bag wrong sides together and,

The warm, earthy colours chosen for the embroidery contrast beautifully with the cool tone of the blue fabric.

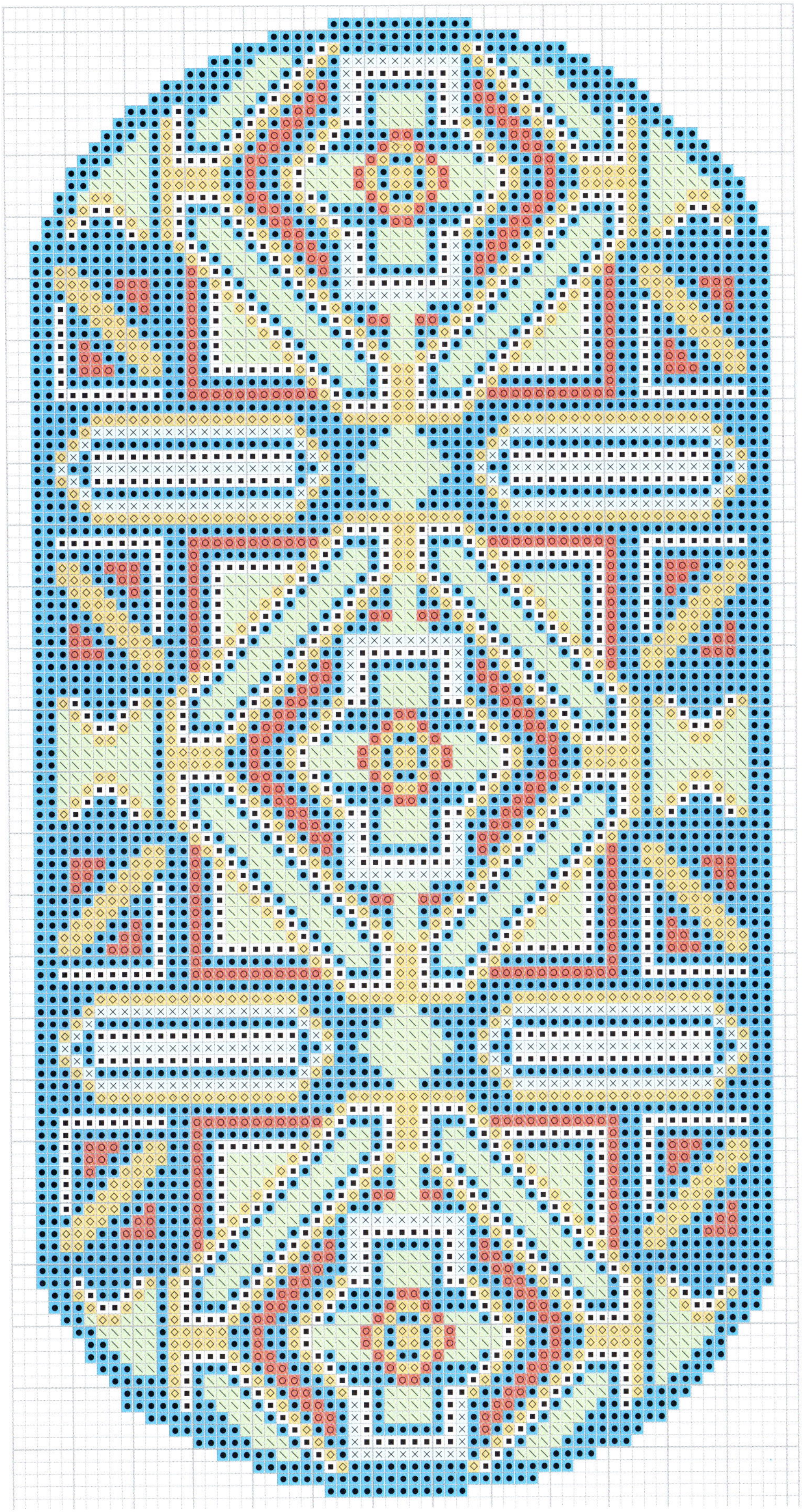

Make-up bag

DMC colour key

7299	Navy
7052	Orange
7314	Blue
7342	Green
1530	White
7606	Red

turning under the seam allowance, hand stitch the lining to the zipper along the stitching lines.

2 Carefully stitch navy cotton cord around each side of the gusset, all around the bag.

GLASSES CASE

EMBROIDERY

1 Cut a piece of canvas 25 x 15 cm and work the tapestry in tent stitch (see chart on page 57).

2 When the tapestry is complete, you will need to block it. Steam the canvas lightly but do not allow the iron to touch the surface of the work. Pull gently into shape and trim the canvas to size, allowing a 1.5 cm seam allowance.

MAKING THE CASE

1 Cut a piece of brocade the same size and shape as the worked canvas. With right sides together, machine sew the canvas to the brocade across the bottom, making sure you stitch along the edge of the worked portion of canvas.

2 Open out the canvas/brocade piece and cut a piece of polypoplin and a piece of wadding the same size.

3 Hand baste the wadding to the wrong side of the canvas/brocade piece and trim to size. With right sides together, pin the lining to the canvas and brocade. Machine stitch together, leaving a 5 cm opening for turning. Trim the edges to 6 mm and notch the turning points to reduce bulk.

TO FINISH

1 Turn the lining through to its right side. Take a piece of cord and sew it invisibly into place around one of the pointed ends.

2 Fold the case so that the pointed ends meet and ladder stitch the sides.

3 Take another piece of cord, tuck one end into the opening, and bind all around the remaining edge. If desired, stitch a velcro dot neatly to each point about 1 cm from the edges.

Making up the glasses case

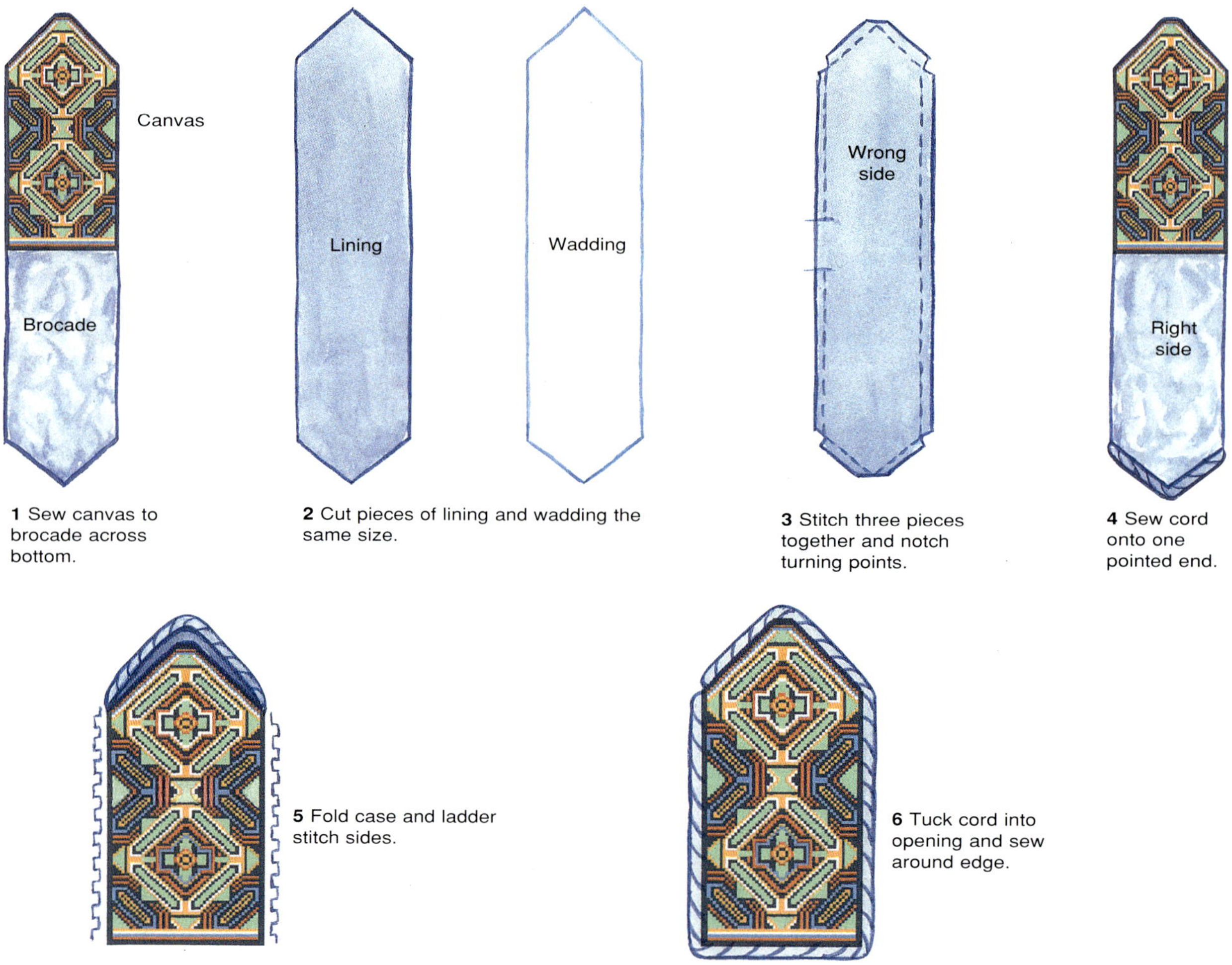

1 Sew canvas to brocade across bottom.

2 Cut pieces of lining and wadding the same size.

3 Stitch three pieces together and notch turning points.

4 Sew cord onto one pointed end.

5 Fold case and ladder stitch sides.

6 Tuck cord into opening and sew around edge.

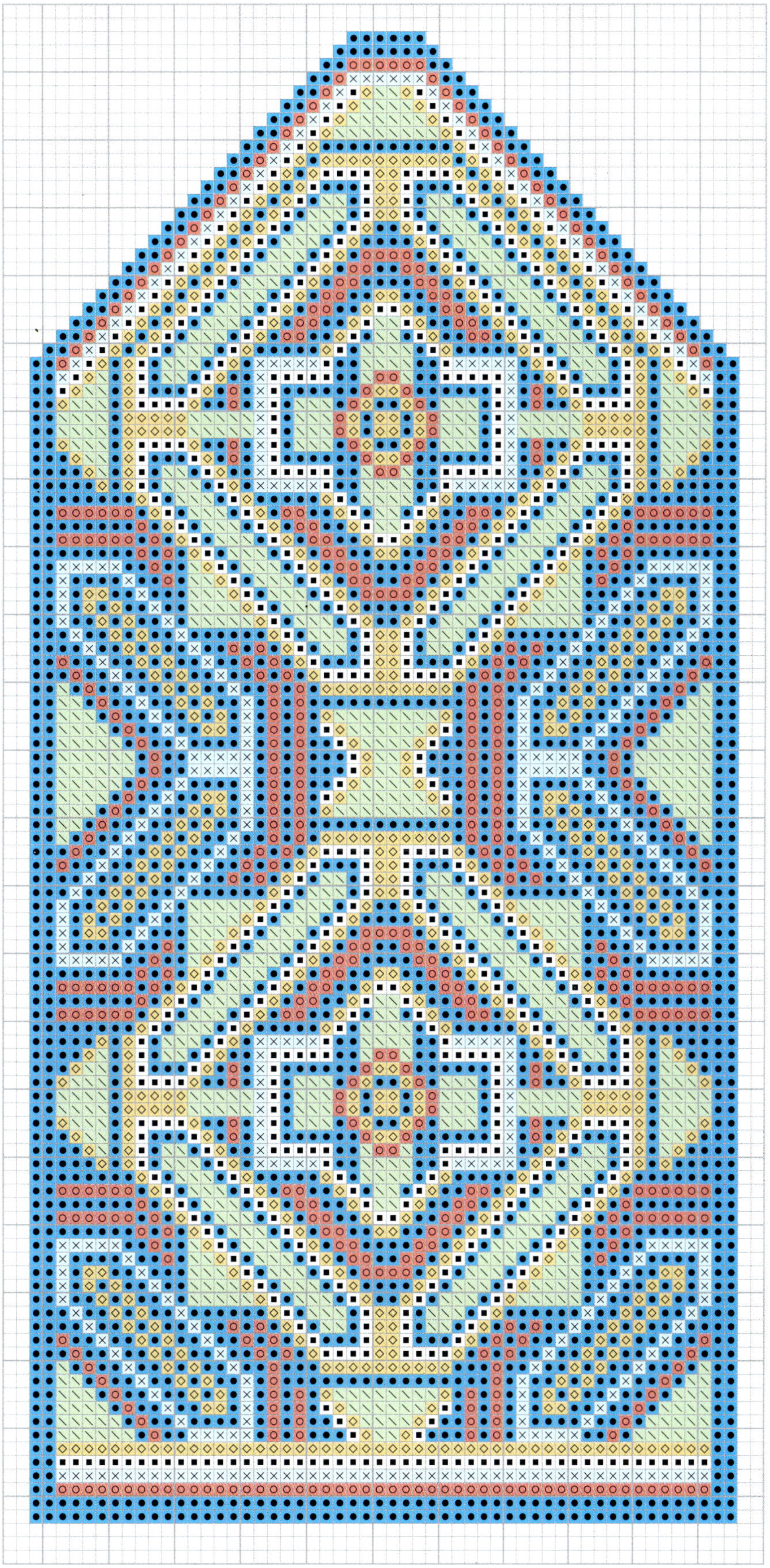

Glasses case

DMC colour key

7299	Navy
7052	Orange
7314	Blue
7342	Green
1530	White
7606	Red

White wedding

Traditional kloster blocks are worked on this elegant Hardanger pouch to create a classic pattern.

Embroider these beautiful keepsakes for the bride and she will feel extra special. Make a handy pouch, a pretty handkerchief and, of course, the essential garter with a touch of blue.

HARDANGER WEDDING POUCH

Finished size 14.5 x 14 cm (maximum height and width, not including hanging ribbon)

Stitches

Algerian eyelet stitch
Needle weaving
Satin stitch
Straight loops

Materials

- Two 20 cm squares of white Belfast linen with 13 threads to 1 cm
- Three 20 cm squares of white satin
- DMC Coton Perlé no. 8 and 12 in white
- Tapestry needles sizes 24 and 26
- Fine crewel needle
- Lightweight iron-on vilene
- Approximately 75 cm of narrow decorative braid
- 26 cm of 1 cm wide satin ribbon
- Crystal or pearl button
- Embroidery hoop
- Small, sharp embroidery scissors
- Tracing paper and pencil

EMBROIDERY

1 Zigzag or overcast one of the linen squares and mark the centre lines vertically and horizontally with a running stitch.

2 Place the linen into the embroidery hoop to keep the work under tension. Using the no. 8 Coton Perlé and size 24 needle, work kloster blocks around the outline of the heart as shown in the chart (see page 60). Kloster blocks are the basis of Hardanger embroidery and each block consists of five satin stitches worked over four threads. The blocks surround the cutwork area. See page 111.

3 With the no. 12 Coton Perlé and size 26 needle, work Algerian eyelets in the centre of each kloster block square. Separate the linen threads in the exact middle of the square and bring the needle up through the centre. Keep the cotton tight enough to open a central hole and work over each linen thread at the base of the satin stitches, bringing the needle up through the centre for each new stitch.

4 With the same cotton and needle begin needleweaving at the point indicated by the first arrow at the top left-hand corner of the design and continue in the direction shown, that is, down one bar, across to the next, down again and so on. The return journey is as indicated by the arrows and the straight loops are worked as the fourth bar is woven. If a new working thread is needed partway along a journey, lay the cotton along the bar and catch one thread of linen from the block where weaving is to begin, then needle weave across the bar, catching in

RIGHT A variety of embroidery techniques are used to make this wedding set a match for a princess: from Hardanger cutwork, to white-on-white shadow work, to pretty grub rose buds.

the new strand. To finish off the cotton along a journey, thread it into a fine crewel needle and run it through the back of one or two woven bars.

5 Carefully cut the linen threads held by the kloster blocks in one third of the design, from the left, and gently withdraw enough lengths of linen thread to work three diagonal rows of straight loops, following the chart. When finished, cut and withdraw more threads and work the next two or three diagonal rows of straight loops. Finally, cut and withdraw the threads to complete the design.

6 When finished, gently wash the embroidered piece to remove all traces of perspiration or soiling. Remove the excess moisture by pressing the embroidery between the folds of a towel. Iron on the wrong side while it is still damp.

HINT

If a linen thread breaks while you're pulling it out, gently remove it and smooth out any gathers. Use a pin to pick up the unbroken end and continue.

MAKING UP THE POUCH

1 Trace the heart shape pattern (see page 105) onto paper and cut it out. Pin the wrong side of the embroidered linen to the right side of one satin square. Position the paper heart template over the linen, placing the centre line of the template over the centre of the embroidery and making sure there is an

Wedding pouch chart

even border of plain linen all around the design. Pin the template securely to the linen and with reasonably small stitches tack around the edge of the heart through the linen and satin to mark the stitching line.
2 Remove the template. Reposition the template on the satin side and mark 5 mm all around for the cutting line. Note the asterisks (*) used in the pattern to denote openings. Remove the template.
3 Place the right side of the embroidery onto the right side of a second satin square and pin carefully close to the heart. Machine stitch on the tacking line through the three pieces of fabric, except from * to * which is to be left as an opening.
4 Cut around the cutting line previously marked. Cut small Vs from the seam edge on curves and cut down to the stitching line at the V at the top of the heart. Snip across the point at the bottom of the heart. Turn inside out, turn in the edges of the opening and ladder stitch together. Lightly press the seam edge.
5 Trace the heart shape onto a piece of vilene, cut out and iron onto the wrong side of the second linen square, being careful to have the heart on the straight grain of the fabric. Pin the linen onto the third satin square, right sides together, and machine stitch around the edge of the vilene, except from * to *. Measure 5 mm from the stitching line all around and cut in the same way as for the first heart. Turn inside out, ladder stitch the opening and lightly press.
6 Ladder stitch the two hearts together leaving the top open from + to +. Slip stitch narrow braid along the edge of the back piece from + to +, then all around the front piece, beginning at the bottom point of the heart and covering the ends of the braid stitched to the back.
7 Attach a button to the front above the embroidery and work a buttonhole loop from the V of the back heart. Stitch a 1 cm hem at each end of the satin ribbon and attach to the inside of the curved tops of the front heart.

Handkerchief motif

HANDKERCHIEF

Finished size Embroidered motif approximately 6 x 3.5 cm

Stitches
Back stitch
Bullion stitch
Detached chain stitch
Double back stitch

Materials
- One lace-edged, undecorated handkerchief
- DMC stranded embroidery cotton in white
- Crewel needle size 9
- HB pencil

METHOD
1 Place the motif in one corner of the handkerchief and lightly trace with the pencil.
2 Use one strand of white embroidery cotton to work the heart in double back stitch, the stems in back stitch and the leaves in detached chain stitch. For the rose buds, work one bullion stitch of 10 wraps for the centre and two bullion stitches of 12 wraps along each side (see the diagram on page 69).
3 Lightly dampen the handkerchief and iron on the wrong side.

SATIN GARTER

Finished size Embroidered motif approximately 4 x 1.5 cm

Stitches
Back stitch
Bullion stitch
Detached chain stitch

Materials
- Strip of white satin 8.5 cm wide and at least twice as long as the elastic needed for the leg size
- DMC stranded embroidery cotton in blue (809)
- Crewel needle size 9
- 2 cm wide elastic
- 6 cm of 2 cm wide white tape or ribbon
- HB pencil

METHOD

1 Trace the motif in the centre of the satin strip, 2.5 cm from each of the long sides. Work with one strand of blue (809) stranded cotton. For the rose buds work one bullion stitch of 10 wraps for the centre and two bullion stitches of 12 wraps for the outside (see the diagram on page 69). Use detached chain stitch to work the leaves and back stitch to work the stems. Press the embroidery carefully on the wrong side of the satin.

2 Bring the strip's long sides together, wrong side out. Machine stitch 5 mm from the edge but leave 4.5 cm behind the embroidery unstitched. Turn to the right side.

3 Turn in the ends of the tube and slip stitch each end to the other, being careful to stitch around the tube, not through it. Press the tube so that the seam lies across the middle of the back.

4 Machine stitch along the long sides of the tube, 5 mm from the edges, but leave an opening above and below the embroidered centre.

5 Cut the elastic to length. Sew the piece of white tape or ribbon to one end of the elastic, overlapping the two pieces by 8 mm. This tape will lie behind the embroidery so that the area is not gathered. Thread the elastic end into the garter through the centre opening and pin the tape end to the back of the tube to make sure it is not pulled through. Pull enough elastic through to eventually join the tape, overlap the edges and stitch the two together, ensuring the tape lies neatly behind the embroidery. Machine stitch down each side of the embroidery and slip stitch the opening closed.

Garter motif

FABRICS

Fabrics used for embroidery are usually divided into two kinds: plainweave and evenweave fabrics. Plain, tightly woven fabrics of linen, cotton or silk are suitable for most surface stitchery. Evenweave fabrics, also known as canvas, are made from wool, linen, cotton, hemp or jute in a regular grid of various sizes so that threads can easily be counted.

These are some of the fabrics used for the projects in this book:

- *Linen.* An evenweave fabric woven from flax. The threads are easily counted.
- *Handkerchief linen.* A very fine linen.
- *Aida cloth.* This evenweave fabric is woven into blocks to give squares for stitching. It comes in a variety of colours and is referred to by the number of squares per inch: 11, 14, 16 and 18 count or squares to the inch.
- *Homespun cotton.* A plainweave cotton fabric made to resemble the fabric made at home.
- *Organza.* A thin, stiff fabric that can be made of silk, cotton, nylon or other fibres.
- *Satin.* Plainweave silk or rayon fabric closely woven to show mainly warp threads and passed through rollers giving a glossy appearance.

A touch of romance is added with these bullion stitch rose buds worked in blue cotton on the satin garter.

Tapestry door buffer

The pansies design on this door buffer is worked in tent stitch using tapestry wool on mono canvas.

Noisy slamming doors will be a thing of the past when you use this beautiful door buffer. The pansy design is worked in tent stitch.

Finished size 20 x 12 cm with each tie about 20 cm

Stitches

Straight stitch
Tent stitch

Materials

- 25 x 30 cm of 14-count mono canvas
- DMC Laine Colbert tapestry wool: navy (7299), yellow (7973), maroon (7212), mauve (7241), light purple (7709), dark purple (7708), lipstick pink (7600), light green (7341), medium green (7342),
- dark green (7344), black
- Madeira metallic thread no. 40 in gold (6)
- 25 x 30 cm of navy fabric
- Tapestry needle
- Tapestry frame
- 2.5 m of gold cord
- Four gold beads
- Polyester toy filling
- Navy sewing thread
- PVA adhesive
- Adhesive tape and scissors

METHOD

1 Following the chart (see page 65), work the background and pansies design in tent stitch. Use navy (7299) wool for the background. Work twelve rows of background at the top and bottom of the design (counting from the highest and lowest points) and seventeen rows on either side. Use gold Madeira thread to work three straight stitches from the yellow centre of each flower.

2 When the tapestry is complete, you will need to block it. Steam it lightly, but do not allow the iron to touch the surface of the work. Moisten the canvas thoroughly enough to enable you to pull it gently into shape.

Door buffer chart

3 Cut two pieces of navy fabric 22 x 9 cm. With their right sides together machine stitch 4 cm at each end, approximately 1.5 cm from the top edge (thus leaving a slit in the seam). Press the seam open.

4 Place the tapestry and the navy fabric (with the seam across the centre) right sides together and sew around 1.5 cm from all edges. Trim the seams to 7 mm. Turn the work through to the right side and gently push the corners out until they are even (they will be slightly rounded). Fill the buffer with polyester filling and invisibly sew up the centre seam.

5 Measure a piece of gold cord the length of the buffer's short sides. Before cutting, wrap adhesive tape around the two ends to stop them fraying. Repeat the process to cut another piece. The tape will be left in place on the finished article.

6 Take the remaining cord and cut it in half. Thread a bead onto each end and tie a knot beneath it leaving 1 cm of cord hanging freely. Apply a dab of PVA adhesive to the bottom of the bead to hold it tightly against the knot. Gently pull the gold wrapping off the 1 cm of cord to create a small tassel.

LEFT The rich, deep colours of tapestry wool, and the added brilliance of metallic gold thread, make this practical door buffer an attractive accessory for any home.

7 Using the gold Madeira thread, stitch the short cords on the short sides of the buffer first, then centre the remaining cords on the long edges. Stitch invisibly along the edge taking care that the gold stitches do not show. When you come to the corners, form a loop with the cord and sew it invisibly over the corner. This hides the ends of the shorter cords.

THREADING THE NEEDLE

Next time you're having a hard time threading a needle, try these handy hints.

- Turn the needle around and insert the thread through the other side. Because the eye of a needle is created by punching it out of the metal, one side is actually bigger than the other.
- Moisten the end of the thread so as to thin out any fraying.
- Twist and fold the end of the thread before threading it through. This is particularly useful when working with wool, but can also be helpful when using stranded cotton.
- Good lighting is essential! Always work either in bright daylight or, if working at night, use a good table lamp with a daylight bulb to cast a clear light that won't hurt your eyes.

Matching tea towel and pot holders

A tea towel and pot holder are essential items in any kitchen. This matching set, with its lovely golden shades, will also be a pleasure to display.

Finished size Tea towel 73 x 49 cm; pot holders 22.5 cm square

Stitches

Satin stitch
Straight stitch

Materials

- Two unprinted good quality linen tea towels approximately 73 x 49 cm
- DMC variegated stranded cotton: two skeins yellow gold (108)
- Tapestry needle size 26
- Two 22 cm squares of padding
- 4 cm wide fabric strips for bias binding
- Machine thread and scissors

Embroidery chart

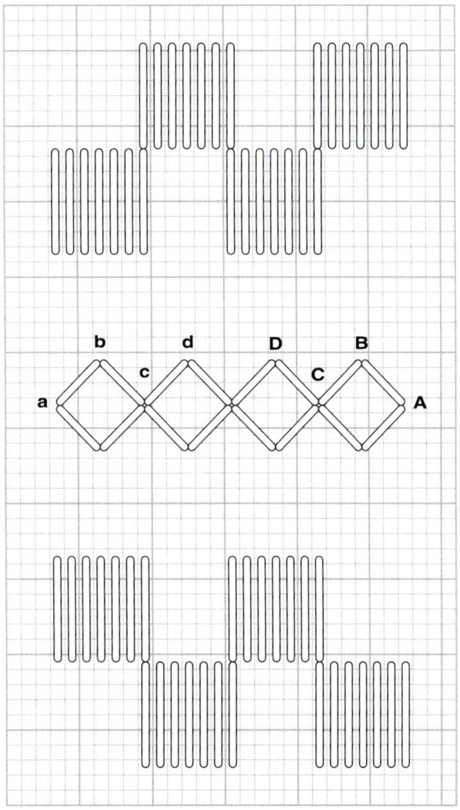

TEA TOWEL

1 Separate three strands of cotton, then realign, ensuring they do not twist together. Approximately 3 cm from the bottom edge of a tea towel, work a double row of satin stitch blocks, each block consisting of seven stitches covering seven horizontal linen threads. Work the two rows as one, beginning each block from the last stitch of the previous block, so that there are six linen threads between each block.
2 Leave seven horizontal linen threads between the rows of blocks and the diamonds. The diamonds are made from two rows of straight stitches slanting across three horizontal and three vertical linen threads and each row is worked in two journeys. For the first journey, bring the needle up at A, across and down at B, under the fabric across and up three threads at C, down at D, and so on. For the second journey, bring the needle up at a, down at b, up at c, down at d, and so on. The third and fourth journeys are worked in a similar fashion to complete the diamonds.
3 Count seven horizontal linen threads from the points of the diamonds and work another set of satin stitch blocks.

POT HOLDERS

1 Cut four 22 cm squares from a tea towel.
2 Zigzag or overcast the edges of two of the squares and embroider these in the same way as the tea towel.
3 Press the squares on the wrong side. Place a square of padding between one embroidered and one plain linen square and baste close to the edge, curving each corner.
4 Machine or hand quilt a 10 cm square in the centre of each pot holder.
5 Make tabs from the bias binding. Place these on a corner, then bind the edges.

HINT

If you have some thin, old towels lying around your house, cut them up into pieces—they make excellent padding for pot holders.

RIGHT Using variegated cotton is a quick and easy way to achieve a striking blend of varying colour tones.

Potpourri

Fragrant sachets

Whether you are an experienced embroiderer or a recent enthusiast, you will enjoy making these simple but charming fragrant sachets. From bullion roses and cutwork, to colonial knots and shadow work, you will be able to practise a variety of techniques to achieve very different effects.

Pretty, yellow grub roses are complemented here by golden leaves worked in detached chain stitch.

YELLOW ROSES BAG

Finished size 10 x 16 cm

Stitches

Bullion stitch
Detached chain stitch
Feather stitch
Fly stitch
Stem stitch

Materials

- 12 x 41 cm of embroidery linen
- DMC stranded embroidery cotton: dark yellow (742), medium yellow (726), light yellow (3078), dark gold (420), medium gold (833), light gold (3046)
- Crewel needles: mixed pack size 5/9
- 70 cm of fine cord
- Small embroidery hoop
- Dried lavender
- Four beads
- Small amount of polyester filling
- Machine thread to match linen
- Sharp lead pencil

LEFT These pretty sachets are perfect as gifts or small tokens of appreciation. Lavender and potpourri are used here, but you can use any other favourite flower or herb to release a delicate and delicious aroma.

Yellow roses motif

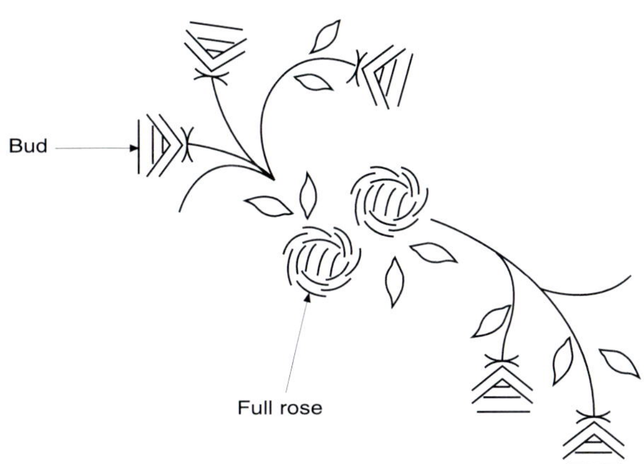

Bullion rose

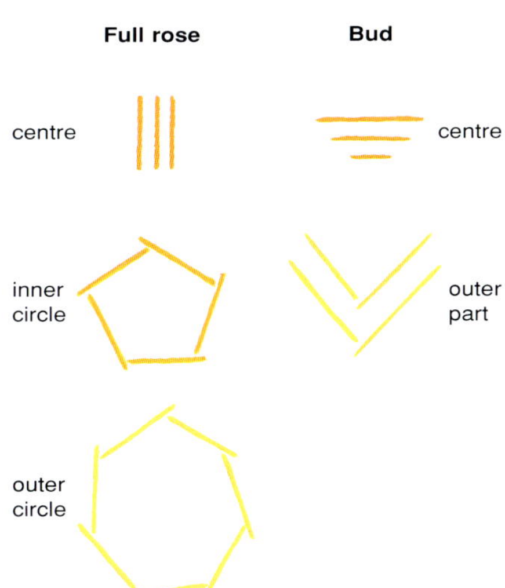

EMBROIDERY

1 Fold the linen in half and press lightly to make the base line.
2 Using a sharp lead pencil, trace the design (see page 69) onto the fabric by taping the design and then the fabric to a window. Position the base of the design 3 cm above the crease line. Trace only the stems and mark a dot for the rose centres and base of the leaves.
3 Overlock around all the raw edges.
4 Place the linen into the embroidery hoop and work the design. Work the two full roses first. The roses are worked in two strands of cotton. Work the centre in dark yellow (742) cotton in bullion stitch of eight wraps; the inner circle in medium yellow (726) in bullion stitch of eight wraps; and the outer circle in light yellow (3078) in bullion stitch of nine wraps.
5 Using one strand of dark gold (420) cotton, embroider the stems in stem stitch and the calyx in two fly stitches.
6 For the buds, use two strands of medium yellow (726) cotton for the centre, working downwards with a bullion stitch of seven wraps, then six and five. For the outer part use light yellow (3078) cotton in bullion stitch of eight wraps.
7 Work the leaves in detached chain stitch, using two strands of medium gold (833) cotton for the large leaves and one strand of light gold (3046) for the small leaves.

MAKING UP THE BAG

1 Press the finished embroidery on the wrong side only. Place the right sides of the bag together, allow a 1 cm seam allowance and machine the side seams.
2 Turn down a 4.5 cm hem allowance and press.
3 To make the casings, sew three rows of machine stitch around the hem, placing the first row 5 mm above the overlocked edge, the second 1 cm above that, and the third a further 1 cm above.

TO FINISH

1 Using two strands of light gold (3046) cotton, feather stitch around the top of the bag and up the side seams as far as the casing.
2 Undo the stitching of the side seams between the first and second rows of stitching on one side and between the second and third rows on the other side. This is to thread the cord through.
3 Cut the cord in half. Thread one half through one opening and out through the same opening. Thread the other half through the other side opening and out through the same opening.
4 Attach the beads to each end of each cord.
5 Place the lavender in the bottom of the bag with a small amount of polyester filling on top, then pull the cords to close the bag.

CUTWORK SACHET

Finished size 10 x 16 cm

Stitches

Buttonhole stitch
Running stitch
Stem stitch

Materials

- White handkerchief lawn (or other closely woven fabric) approximately 25 x 22 cm
- DMC Coton Perlé no.12 in white
- Crewel needle size 9
- Small tapestry needle
- Stiletto
- Potpourri
- 1 cm wide mauve ribbon
- White machine thread
- Small, sharp-pointed scissors and HB pencil

The outline of this floral design is worked in running stitch first, then in buttonhole stitch. The effect is enhanced with a piece of lavender-coloured paper placed behind the embroidery.

Cutwork sachet motif

EMBROIDERY

1 Fold the fabric in half to make a piece 12.5 x 22 cm and lightly press the fold.

2 Open out the fabric and with a pencil trace the outline of the design, the flowers, leaves and eyelets (but not the bars), centring the design across the crease and approximately 4 cm above the bottom raw edge. Draw scallops (about 2 cm wide and 0.5 cm deep) approximately 17 cm from the bottom edge of the material.

3 To work the scalloped edge, use running stitch along the outline with the Coton Perlé and crewel needle; then work over the running stitches in buttonhole stitch, using the tapestry needle.

4 With the Coton Perlé and crewel needle, embroider the flower and leaves following the outline first in running stitch and then in buttonhole stitch with the tapestry needle. Work the veins within the flowers and leaves in stem stitch with the crewel needle.

5 For the centre eyelets, make a small circle of running stitches using the crewel needle. Make a hole with the stiletto, then overcast around the hole.

6 For the larger outer eyelets make a larger circle of running stitches and cut slits inside it with small, sharp-pointed scissors.

Eyelet slit 

Fold the material back as you buttonhole stitch around the circle using the crewel needle.

7 To embroider the bars, use the crewel needle and anchor the threads. For each bar, start the threads at the left-hand side, then make a small stitch at the right-hand side, and then one at the left-hand side again. Switch to the tapestry needle and work buttonhole stitches over these bars, taking care that the stitches do not enter the material except for one or two stitches at each end to anchor the bars so that they don't pull away when the background is cut. Once the fabric is cut away, a buttonholed 'bridge' will be left.

8 When all the embroidery is finished, press the work and then, using small, sharp-pointed scissors, carefully cut away the fabric below the 'bridges'. Trim carefully around the scalloped edges also.

MAKING UP THE BAG

1 Fold the fabric along the previous crease so that the sides meet, right sides out. Make a small French seam at the back.

2 With the sachet's right sides together, place the French seam at the centre of the back and press lightly to crease the side folds. Hand baste the bottom edges together and stitch through all layers in a narrow seam. Trim the seam if necessary and overlock or zigzag to neaten off. Turn to right side.

TO FINISH

Insert a small pillow of potpourri cased in lawn and tie with a ribbon. Coloured paper has been slipped behind the design to heighten its effect.

GINGHAM POTPOURRI BAG

Finished size 10 x 16 cm

Stitches

Stem stitch

Materials

- 22 x 16 cm of check gingham
- 20 cm square white cotton fabric
- DMC stranded embroidery cotton in mauve (210)
- Raffia

Gingham potpourri bag lettering

- Potpourri
- Water-erasable pen
- Pinking shears
- Machine thread

EMBROIDERY

1 Fold the gingham in half to make a piece 11 x 16 cm and measure 5 cm up from the bottom. This is the point across which you'll centre your lettering.
2 Trace the lettering (see page 71) onto the gingham with a water-erasable pen.
3 Embroider the lettering in stem stitch using two strands of the mauve (210) cotton.

MAKING UP THE BAG

1 Trim the top of the fabric with pinking shears to create a jagged edge.
2 With right sides together, machine the centre seam down the back of the sachet and across the bottom. Turn to right side.

TO FINISH

1 Make an inner bag with the white fabric and fill it with potpourri. Stitch the bag closed and insert it into the sachet.
2 Tie the sachet with three strands of raffia and make a raffia loop at the back for hanging.

GUM BLOSSOMS ON ORGANZA

Finished size 10 x 16 cm

Stitches

Colonial knot
Long stitch
Stem stitch

Materials

- 30 cm cream organza
- DMC stranded embroidery cotton: green (3052), light apricot (760), dark apricot (351), cream (739)
- Crewel needle size 9
- 15 cm (6 in) embroidery hoop
- Ribbons to match embroidery
- Potpourri
- Machine thread to match organza
- HB pencil

EMBROIDERY

1 From the organza cut a 36 x 26 cm rectangle.
2 Fold the organza in half to make a piece 18 x 26 cm and press the fold. The bag is made from two layers of organza, with the embroidery done on the top layer only. Open out and with a pencil, trace the outline of the design onto one half of the organza, centring it and placing it approximately 4 cm above the raw edge to allow for the hem.
3 Using the embroidery hoop to hold the organza firmly in place, work the leaves and nuts in stem stitch using two strands of green (3052) cotton. Using one strand of each of the apricot cottons (760 and 351), work long stitch for the blossom filaments. Complete by adding colonial knots at the end of the filaments, using the dark apricot (351) cotton.

MAKING UP THE BAG

1 When the embroidery is completed, fold the fabric again along the previous crease, join the sides together right sides out and, treating this double thickness as one (there will be four layers of material at the seam), sew a French seam.
2 With the sachet's right sides together, place the French seam at the centre of the back and press lightly to crease the side folds. Hand baste the bottom edges together and stitch through all layers in a

Gum blossom motif

Tiny colonial knots at the end of each blossom filament perfect this simple, but striking design.

narrow seam. Trim the seam if necessary and overlock or zigzag to neaten off. Turn to right side.

TO FINISH

1 Using the cream (739) cotton, work eight evenly spaced buttonhole bar keepers, approximately 7 mm wide, around the sachet. Place them 1 cm above the top of the design. Thread the ribbons through.

2 Fill the sachet with potpourri and tie knots or bows as preferred.

LAVENDER SHADOW WORK

Finished size 10 x 16 cm

Stitches

Bullion stitch
Double back stitch
Fly stitch
Shell stitch
Stem stitch

Materials

- Piece of mauve voile or muslin 35 x 15 cm
- DMC stranded embroidery cotton: mauve (210), green (368)
- Mauve ribbon 5 mm wide and 50 cm long
- Mauve machine thread to match fabric
- Dried lavender
- Pins

EMBROIDERY

1 Fold the fabric in half to make a piece 17.5 x 15 cm, then press the fold to make a crease. Place the design under one half of the fabric, about 1.5 cm above the crease. Pin in place and trace.

2 One strand of embroidery cotton is used for the design. Double back stitch the bow in mauve (210).

3 In the same colour, work several bullion stitches at the top of the stems to make the flowers.

4 Work stem stitch for the stalks and small fly stitches for the leaves, all in the green (368) cotton. Dampen the fabric and embroidery and press on the wrong side.

MAKING UP THE BAG

1 Trim the width of the fabric to 11 cm, keeping the design in the centre. Fold in half with the embroidery inside, machine 5 mm seams and zigzag or overlock the edges. Shell stitch a narrow hem at the top with the mauve machine thread.

2 Find the mid-point of the ribbon and sew it to the middle of the back of the sachet, 5 cm from the hem.

TO FINISH

Fill the sachet with dried lavender and tie the ribbon in a bow.

Lavender motif

Bargello 'in the round' sewing set

This captivating pattern is worked almost entirely in stab stitch.

Bargello embroidery produces an interesting, eye-catching effect, enhanced in this handy sewing set by the varying shades of brilliant colours.

Finished size Sewing pouch 14 x 14 cm; needle case 10 x 10 cm; pin cushion 8 x 8 cm; scissors anchor 3 x 3 cm (all when finished)

Stitches

Long-legged cross stitch
Stab stitch

Materials

- Interlock canvas with 18 holes to 2.5 cm
- DMC Coton Perlé no. 3: two skeins each lavender (211), light violet (554), medium violet (552), dark violet (550); one skein each baby pink (818), medium pink (761), dark pink (760), deep rose (309), light blue (800), medium blue (799), dark blue (798), royal blue (796)
- Tapestry needle size 22
- 2 cm wide masking tape or bias binding
- Lining fabric
- White and pink machine threads
- Soft felt or flannel
- Small piece of pink grosgrain ribbon or fabric strip
- Small quantity of polyester filling
- Two press studs
- Two small buttons
- A few fancy beads (optional)
- Pinking shears
- Scissors and HB pencil

EMBROIDERY

1 Find the exact centre of the canvas and mark the hole with a pencil. Carefully mark the diagonals from the centre hole by jumping the pencil from hole to hole for a few centimetres, not ruling a line as it may be inaccurate. After stitching several rounds of the design you will be able to follow the diagonals easily.

2 Work by stab stitching down and up, keeping the tension firm but not tight, and with the needle perpendicular to the canvas. Work with the cotton no longer than 45–50 cm. If the cotton begins to flatten, twirl the needle several times to regain twist. If you need to unpick some stitches, do not reuse the cotton.

3 When beginning a row, leave a short 'tail' of cotton to be secured at the back by covering it with stitches. When you finish a row, run the needle through the back of a few stitches to secure the thread.

4 Work begins at the centre of the design and is worked in rounds across four quarters (see chart on page 76). At the diagonal, the stitches are worked at right angles to the previous ones. The chart shows the first five rows of the design. Rows 1, 2 and 3 each have stitches covering a different number of canvas threads to the previous row to establish the pattern. Row 4 begins with three stitches at the diagonal and covers four canvas threads all round. Row 5 and all rows thereafter begin with four stitches and cover four canvas threads all round.

5 Follow the corner chart on page 77 for finishing the corners on the last row.

SEWING POUCH

1 Cut a 26 x 26 cm piece of canvas and bind the edges with masking tape or sew on bias binding.

2 Using the lavender and violet cottons, follow the steps in 'Embroidery'. Work eighteen rows, then a

RIGHT This Bargello embroidery is begun at the centre of the design and worked in rounds.

19th row to fill in the spaces between the stitches in row 18.

3 Trim the canvas back to seven threads from the last row, turn down three threads to the back of the work and overcast the edges all round, mitring the corners.

4 Carefully iron with a damp cloth on the wrong side and block the square if necessary. To block, steam the canvas lightly but do not allow the iron to touch the surface of the work. Pull gently into shape to make a perfect square.

5 Cut the lining to size, turn in the edges and stitch to the base of the overcast row on the canvas.

6 Turn three points of the square in to the centre (creating an envelope) and firmly ladder stitch the sides of these flaps together. Work a buttonhole loop on the point of the fourth flap and attach a button to hold the pouch closed.

NEEDLE CASE

1 Cut a 19 x 19 cm piece of canvas and bind the edges with masking tape or sew on bias binding.

2 Using the pink and rose cottons, follow the steps in 'Embroidery'. Work thirteen rows, then a 14th row to fill in the spaces between the stitches in row 13.

3 Trim the canvas back to six threads from the last row, turn down three threads to the back of the work and overcast the edges all round, mitring the corners.

Embroidery chart

4 Carefully iron with a damp cloth on the wrong side and block the square if necessary. To block, steam the canvas lightly but do not allow the iron to touch the surface of the work. Pull gently into shape to make a perfect square.
5 Cut the lining to size, turn in the edges and stitch to the base of the overcast row on the canvas.
6 With the pinking shears, cut two 8.5 x 8.5 cm squares of felt or flannel. Stitch these onto the centre of the lining with the pink machine thread, ensuring the stitches go through to the centre of the embroidered pattern.
7 Still working on the lined side of the square, sew a piece of grosgrain ribbon or a strip of folded fabric to one corner and stitch press studs on each of the adjacent corners. Bring the three corners to the centre and sew corresponding press studs on the ribbon.
8 Work a buttonhole loop on the point of the fourth flap and attach a button to hold the pouch closed.

PIN CUSHION

1 Cut an 18 x 18 cm piece of canvas and bind the edges with masking tape or sew on bias binding.
2 Using the blue cottons, follow the steps in 'Embroidery'. Work twelve rows, then a 13th row to fill in the spaces between the stitches in row 12.
3 Carefully iron with a damp cloth on the wrong side and block the square if necessary. To block, steam the canvas lightly but do not allow the iron to touch the surface of the work. Pull gently into shape to make a perfect square.
4 Trim the canvas back to five threads from the last row and turn down from the edge of the embroidery all around.

Corner chart

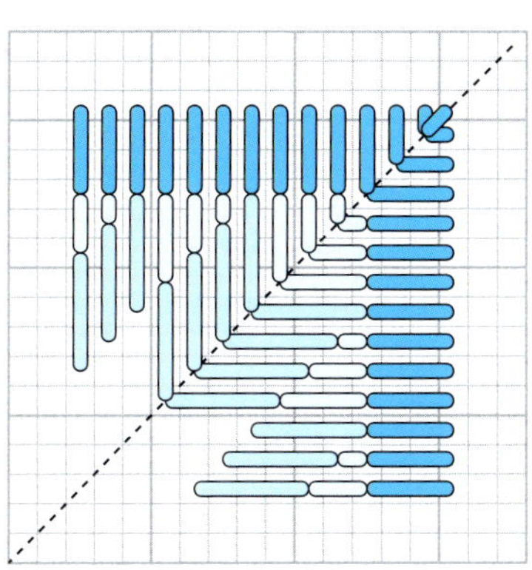

5 Fold the four corners of the square to the centre and, beginning from the base of two of the quarters, work long-legged cross stitches to join the sides. Leave an opening in the last join, stuff the cushion firmly with polyester filling, and complete the closure.

SCISSORS ANCHOR

1 Cut two 5 x 5 cm pieces of canvas and bind the edges with masking tape or sew on bias binding.
2 Find the exact centre of each piece and mark the hole with a pencil. Carefully mark the diagonals from the centre hole by jumping the pencil from hole to hole, not ruling a line as it may be inaccurate. After stitching several rounds of the design you will be able to follow the diagonals easily.
3 Using the lavender and violet cottons, follow the steps in 'Embroidery', but refer to the chart below. Work four rows.
4 Trim the canvas to four threads from the last row and turn down from the edge of the embroidery all around.
5 Use two strands of light violet (554) cotton to make a 23 cm cord. Then take one strand of the same cotton to make a small tassel: wind the strand around three fingers (approximately twelve wraps), slide them out, tie close to one end and snip the other. Decorate the tassel with beads as desired. Attach the cord onto the wrong side of one square's corner, then add the tassel to the opposing corner.
6 Stitch the two squares together with long-legged cross stich but before completing the fourth side, lightly stuff with polyester filling.

Scissors anchor

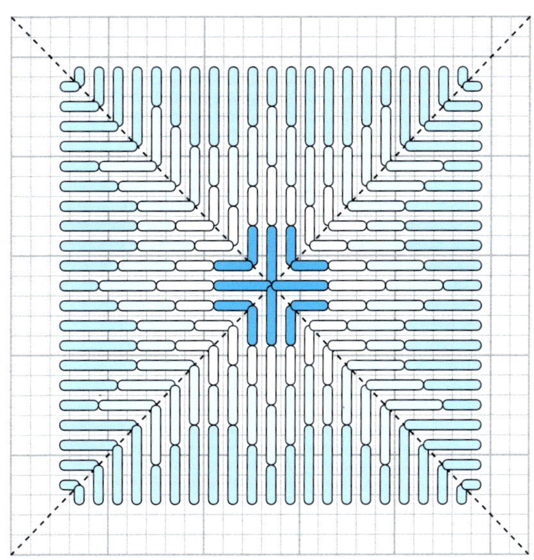

Cross-stitch floral pictures

These lovely cross-stitch pictures are incredibly easy to embroider and look fantastic in rustic wooden frames. Whether you display them separately or together, they are the perfect decorative tool.

Finished size Embroidered area approximately 5.5 cm square

Stitches

Cross stitch

LEFT *Take the unrivalled beauty of primroses, roses and forget-me-nots straight into your home. The delicate qualities of antique blue, dusty rose and pale yellow make these cross-stitch pictures absolute treasures.*

Materials

- Three 18 x 20 cm pieces of 16-count white Aida cloth
- DMC stranded embroidery cotton: white, baby blue (3325), antique blue (932), pistachio green (368), forest green (988), dusty rose (963), medium rose (899), pale yellow (745), tangerine (742), beige-brown (840), medium delft (799), dark delft (798), medium mauve (3688)
- Tapestry needle size 24

METHOD

1 Following the chart, embroider each design in the centre of the Aida cloth. Work cross stitch over one fabric square using two strands of cotton.

2 Frame as desired.

Yellow primroses

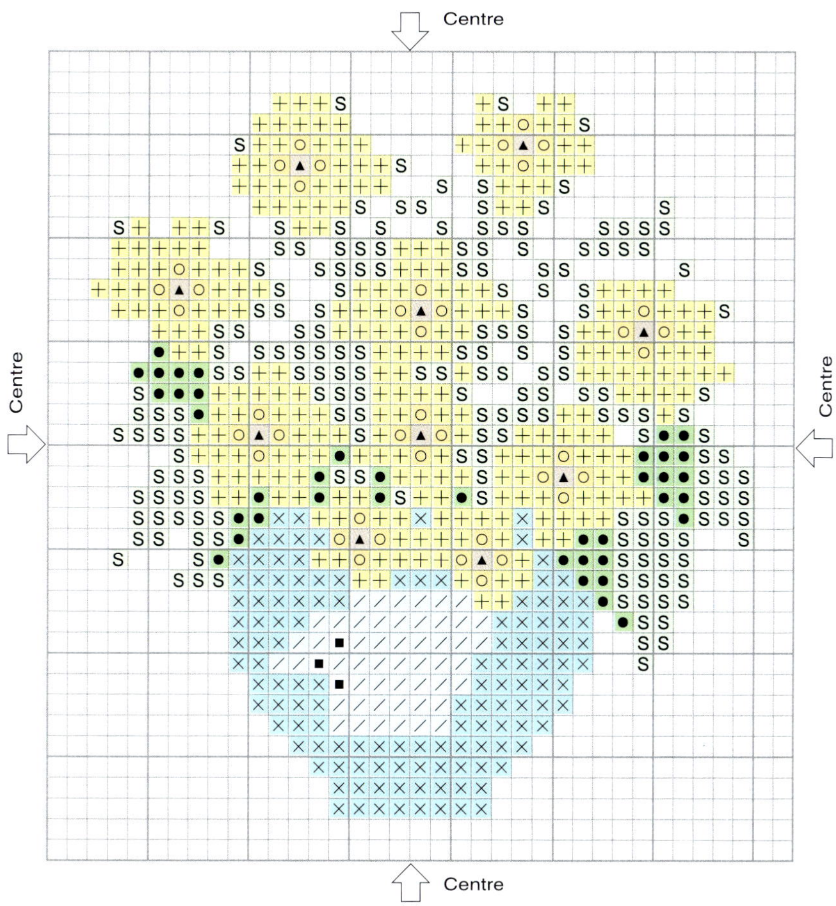

DMC colour key

▪		White
o	742	Tangerine
+	745	Pale yellow
▲	840	Beige-brown
s	368	Pistachio green
●	988	Forest green
×	932	Antique blue
/	3325	Baby blue

Pink roses

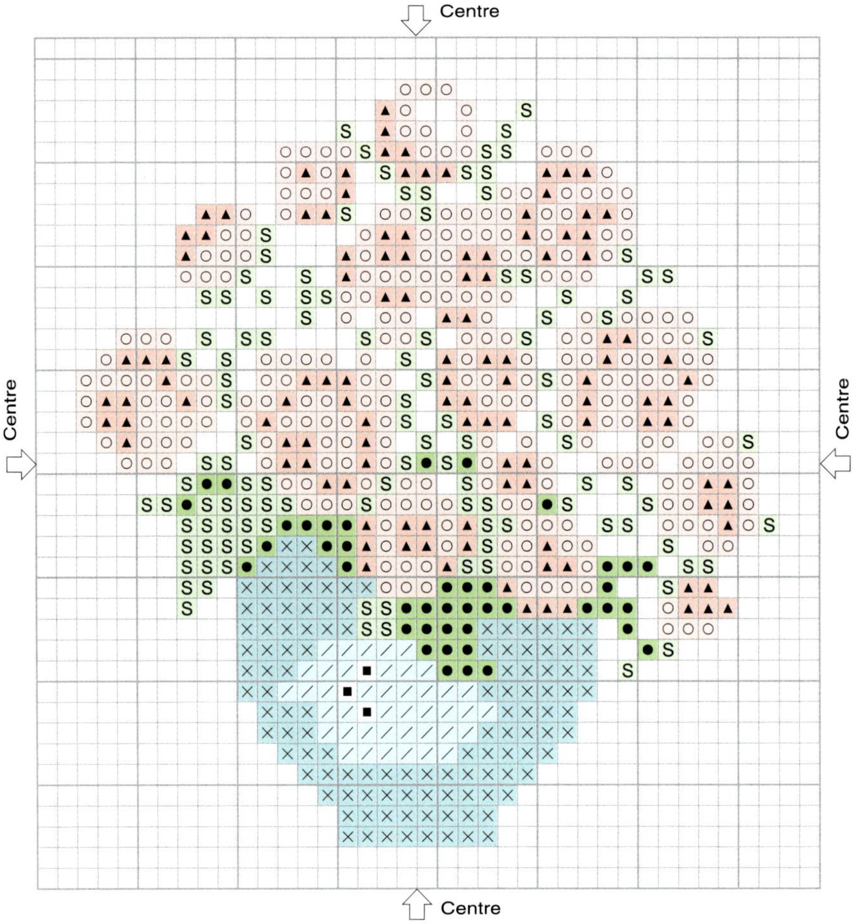

DMC colour key

▪		White
○	963	Dusty rose
▲	899	Medium rose
S	368	Pistachio green
●	988	Forest green
×	932	Antique blue
/	3325	Baby blue

Blue forget-me-nots

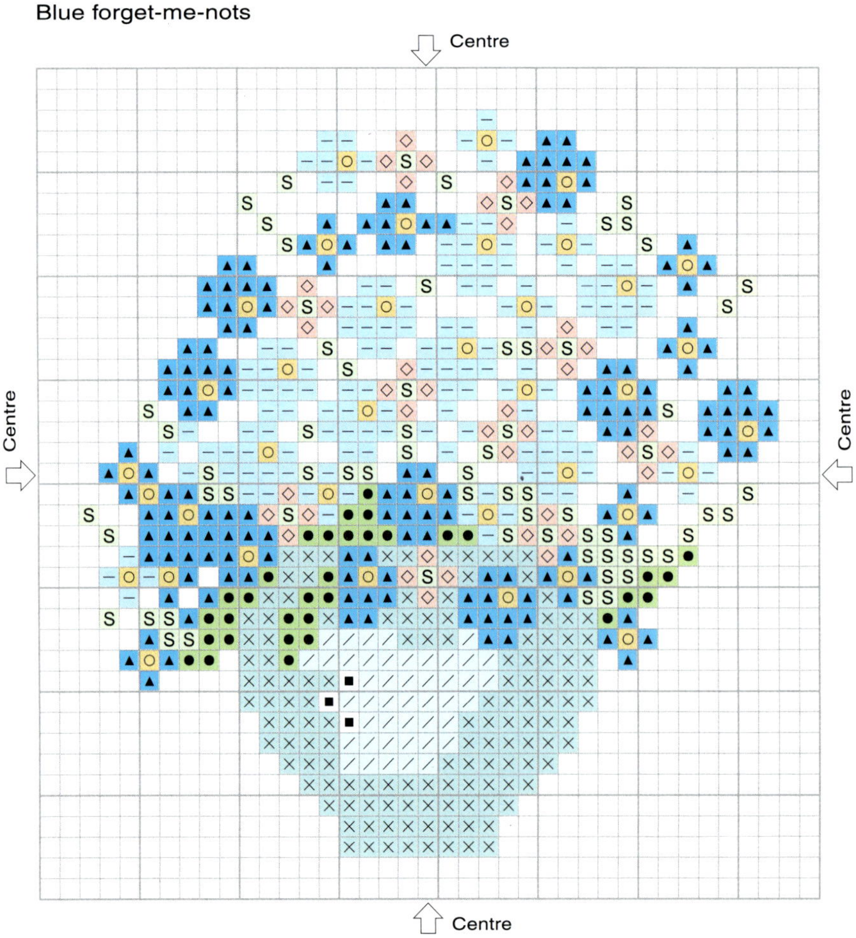

DMC colour key

▪		White
○	742	Tangerine
–	799	Medium delft
▲	798	Dark delft
◇	3688	Medium mauve
S	368	Pistachio green
●	988	Forest green
×	932	Antique blue
/	3325	Baby blue

Embroidered kitchen ensemble

The shelf liner features pretty cutwork flowers and a scalloped edge.

The bright and clear feel of this ensemble is perfect for adding a dash of light to your kitchen. It will complement any kitchen style and is suitable for both casual or more formal settings.

Finished size Shelf liners 29 x 71 cm; breadbasket cloth approximately 35 cm square; egg cosies 7.5 cm wide

Stitches

Buttonhole stitch
Chain stitch
French or colonial knot
Running stitch
Satin stitch
Stem stitch
Straight stitch

Materials

- 70 cm of 115 cm wide white handkerchief linen
- DMC stranded embroidery cotton: white, red (666), green (3346), yellow (973), pink (602), blue (809)
- Crewel needle size 9
- One craft square of white felt
- White machine thread
- Green seed beads (optional)
- Embroidery hoop
- Stiletto
- Very sharp-pointed embroidery scissors
- HB pencil and scrap paper

SHELF LINERS

PREPARATION

1 Measure your shelf to decide on the required width and length of the liner. To these dimensions add approximately 3 cm in length and 5 cm in width. This is to allow for a 1.5 cm hem at the top and sides, and for excess fabric for the scalloped edge. Cut the linen as required.

2 Each scallop measures 12 cm across. If your shelf has odd dimensions you will need to work an incomplete scallop at either end. With a pencil, trace the shelf liner design (see page 83) onto the linen.

EMBROIDERY

1 It is essential to use an embroidery hoop when working this design. Using two strands of white cotton work two rows of chain stitch around the scallops, tapering into the corners. Work over this in buttonhole stitch.

2 Using two strands of green (3346) cotton, work small running stitches around each leaf (see the diagram on page 84). Cut a small slit inside each leaf, leaving the cotton intact. Pass the needle and thread down through the slit and then up, encasing a small amount of material into an overcast edge. Overcast only a couple of threads including the running stitch.

3 Work the stems in stem stitch using two strands of green (3346) cotton.

4 Work the flower petals in the same way as the leaves, alternating between blue (809) and pink (602) flowers across the liner. In the centre of each flower, work six French or colonial knots in two strands of yellow (973) cotton.

5 Work the red (666) eyelets along the edge of the scallops the same way as the leaves and petals, but instead of cutting a slit, gently poke a stiletto down through the centre of the outlined circle, then overcast the edge (see the diagram on page 84).

TO FINISH

1 When the embroidery is complete, wash gently in soapy warm water to remove any pencil marks. Rinse well and dry.

2 Press the work lightly and make a small hand-stitched hem along the remaining three edges. Press using a spray starch, then carefully cut away excess material from around the scalloped edge.

HINT

To hold the liner in place on the shelf, you could glue a velcro dot to the back of the shelf and stitch the corresponding dot to the underside of the embroidered liner.

LEFT Use this cheerful kitchen ensemble to spruce up your own kitchen or make it as the ideal gift for a house warming or kitchen tea. Either way, you'll be impressing your friends.

Breadbasket cloth design

Shelf liner design

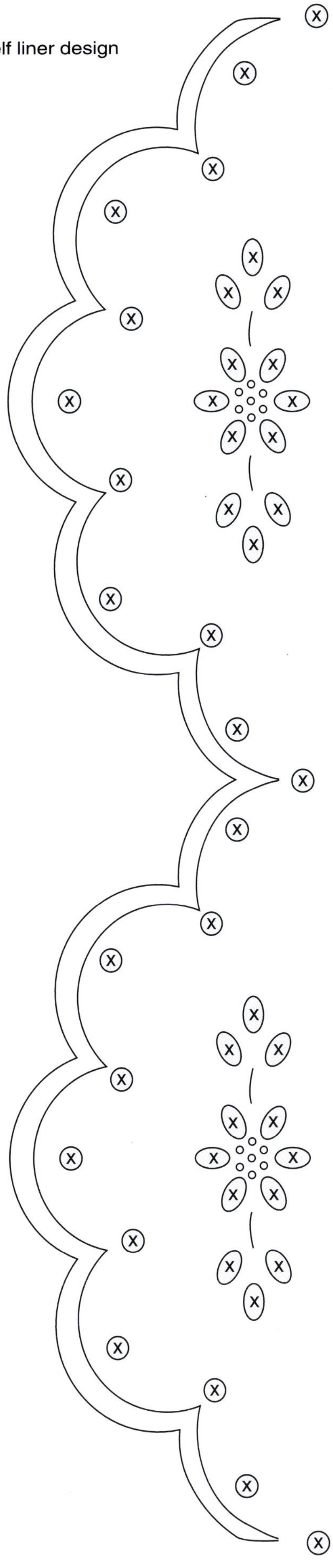

BREADBASKET CLOTH

PREPARATION

1 Cut a piece of linen 40 cm square.

2 With a pencil, trace the flower and scalloped edge design (see page 83) in one corner, about 2.5 cm from the raw edges.

EMBROIDERY

1 It is essential to use an embroidery hoop when working this design. Using two strands of white cotton, work the scallops around the edge, using two rows of chain stitch and tapering into the corners. Work over this in buttonhole stitch.

2 For the flowers, work tiny running stitches around the centre of the flower, its petals, leaves and bud, using two strands of the appropriate colour for each: yellow (973) for the centre, red (666) for the petals, green (3346) for the leaves and pink (602) for the bud. When completed, work two chain stitches within each, again in each corresponding colour as padding for the satin stitch. Satin stitch across each section making sure the stitches are close together and that they cover the padding stitches.

3 Using two strands of blue (809) cotton, work straight stitches between each red petal from the centre of the flower. If you want, stitch a green bead at the end of each.

4 Work the stems in stem stitch using two strands of green (3346) cotton.

TO FINISH

1 When the embroidery is complete, wash gently in soapy warm water to remove any pencil marks. Rinse well and dry.

2 Press the work lightly using a spray starch, then carefully cut away excess material from around the scalloped edge.

TWO EGG COSIES

PREPARATION

1 Cut a piece of linen 35 x 35 cm.

2 With a pencil trace the design with the scalloped edge and flower motif twice onto the linen, placing each approximately 2 cm above the bottom raw edge of the fabric and leaving sufficient room between the designs for cutting out the cosies. Then turn the fabric upside down and, in line with these designs, trace only the scalloped edge and eyelets twice, approximately 2 cm above the raw edge.

Egg cosy pattern and design

Working the leaves

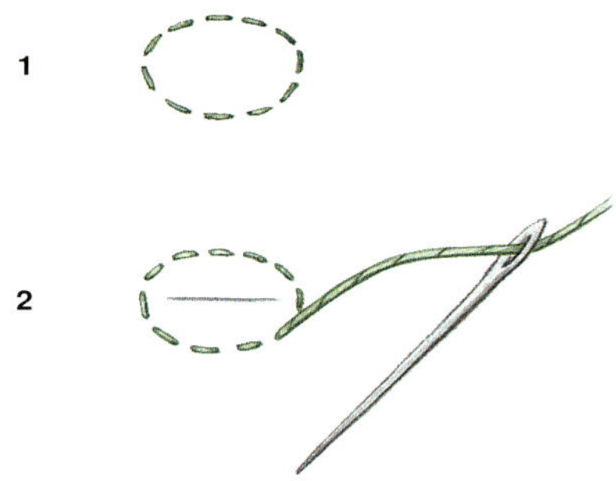

Working the eyelets

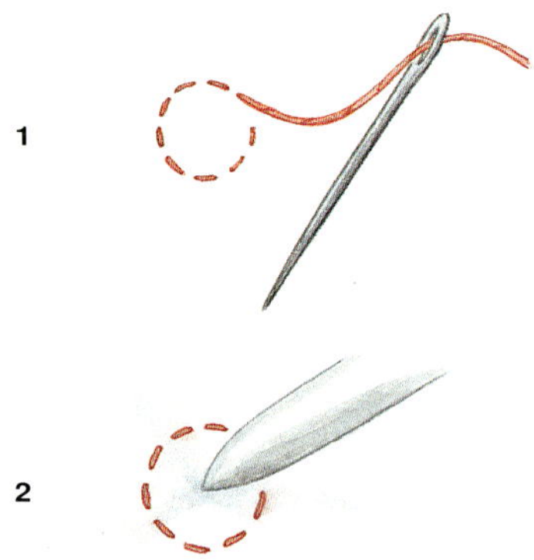

EMBROIDERY

Work the scalloped edge and flower as described for the breadbasket cloth, and the eyelets as described for the shelf liners.

TO FINISH

1 Make a paper pattern for the egg cosy, pin it onto the finished embroidery and cut out two backs and two fronts.

2 Place the back and front pieces together right sides in and hand baste around the edges. Machine stitch around the edges, then trim the seams to about 6 mm and zigzag stitch all around.

3 Turn the right sides out and press the seams flat. Carefully cut the excess linen from around the buttonholed scallops. Spray lightly with spray starch and press.

4 To make the lining, pin the paper pattern onto a piece of felt and cut out four pieces.

5 Put two pieces of felt together and machine stitch around the edges. Do the same for the other two pieces and place each lining inside an egg cosy.

Satin stitch flowers are beautifully enhanced with tiny green seed beads and delicate eyelets.

EMBROIDERY THREADS

There are so many different threads available to the embroiderer, the choice can seem a little daunting. Experimenting with them on a scrap piece of fabric is the best option for getting to know the many different types. The following descriptions might also help.

■ Stranded embroidery cotton (also known as 'floss') is the thread most often used. It is made up of six strands, eight metres long, and is available in many shades of colours. Stranded cotton should be used in lengths of no more than 50 cm or the thread will lose its sheen. Depending on the fineness of the work, one or more strands can be used. Stranded cotton is suitable for many types of embroidery, including counted cross stitch, shadow work, cutwork and all types of surface stitchery.

■ Coton Perlé, or pearl cotton, is a shiny, twisted thread available in skeins or balls. Although its strands are not divisible, the thread comes in various thicknesses—3 (the thickest), 5, 8 and 12 (the thinnest)—and is suitable for many types of embroidery, including cross stitch, tapestry, smocking and Hardanger.

■ Broder cotton is a soft, matt thread, also available in a number of thicknesses—4 (the thickest), 12, 16, 20, 25, 30 and 35 (the thinnest). Numbers 16 and 20 are available in a range of colours, but the finer 25 only in white or ecru. Broder cotton is suitable for all types of embroidery, including canvas work, candlewicking, smocking and cross stitch.

■ Flower Thread also has a matt finish and its soft, muted colours are useful for giving an antique effect to cross stitch embroidery. One strand of Flower Thread is equal to two strands of stranded cotton.

■ Variegated thread is a stranded cotton dyed in shades of one colour by methods such as tie dyeing, which produces a beautiful watercolour wash effect.

■ Art silk can be a little difficult to work with due to its high degree of shine. Made of rayon or viscose, it is commonly used for counted thread embroidery, canvas work and surface stitchery.

■ Tapestry wool is the most common thread for canvas work or tapestry. It is quite easy to work with, but is difficult to separate, so it must fit the scale of the canvas perfectly. For best results, always work a sample first.

Cross-stitch baby set

This beautiful set of matching sheet, pillowcase, bib and birth sampler is the perfect gift for the new mum. Simple to embroider and sew, the set will become a family keepsake.

Finished size Bib 25.5 x 30.5 cm (not including ties); cot sheet 65 x 103 cm (adjust to fit your cot); birth sampler approximately 15.5 cm high (width depends on the length of the name)

Stitches

Back stitch
Cross stitch

Materials

- 1.20 m of check fabric
- DMC stranded embroidery cotton: light blue (828), medium blue (809), dark blue (824), red (666), yellow (973), hunter green (3346), yellow-green (3348), orange (721), light pink (605), dark pink (602), white
- 1 m of Aida cloth
- 30 x 5 cm band of Aida
- 35 cm square of white towelling
- Tapestry needle size 26
- Approximately 1.9 m of piping
- Bias binding (to match piping)
- 15 cm (6 in) embroidery hoop
- Sewing thread

A birth sampler is the ideal way to commemorate baby's special day and makes a wonderful, cherished gift. It's also fantastic for decorating baby's room.

BIRTH SAMPLER

1 Cut a large piece of Aida cloth, ensuring you allow 8 cm of Aida around the edges of the design (see page 88) to enable the picture framer to 'block' the work properly. Overlock the edges to prevent fraying.

2 Find the mid-point of the piece. A simple way of doing this is to fold the cloth in half lengthways, then crossways. Mark the vertical and horizontal lines across the mid-point with sewing thread.

3 Work out the placement of the lettering and the numbers (see pages 90–2), leaving two squares between each character. It may be necessary to change the colour scheme of some of the letters so as to balance out the colours. Work the design in cross stitch from the top down, making sure all your threads cross over in the same direction. Lengthen the horizontal borders to fit the name. Choose the colours for the birth date to complement the name. Work the birth date in two colours only, with the outline in a third strong colour (we used light blue (828) and dark blue (824), with dark pink (602) for the outline). Use two or three strands of cotton, as preferred.

4 Frame as desired.

RIGHT The variety of colours and patterns in this embroidered lettering makes for interesting stitching.

NICHOLAS
BABY

Sampler chart

DMC colour key

●	824	Dark blue
×	809	Medium blue
▲	828	Light blue
o	666	Red
+	973	Yellow
ʌ	3346	Hunter green
\	3348	Yellow-green
◇	721	Orange
S	602	Dark pink
P	605	Light pink
▪		White

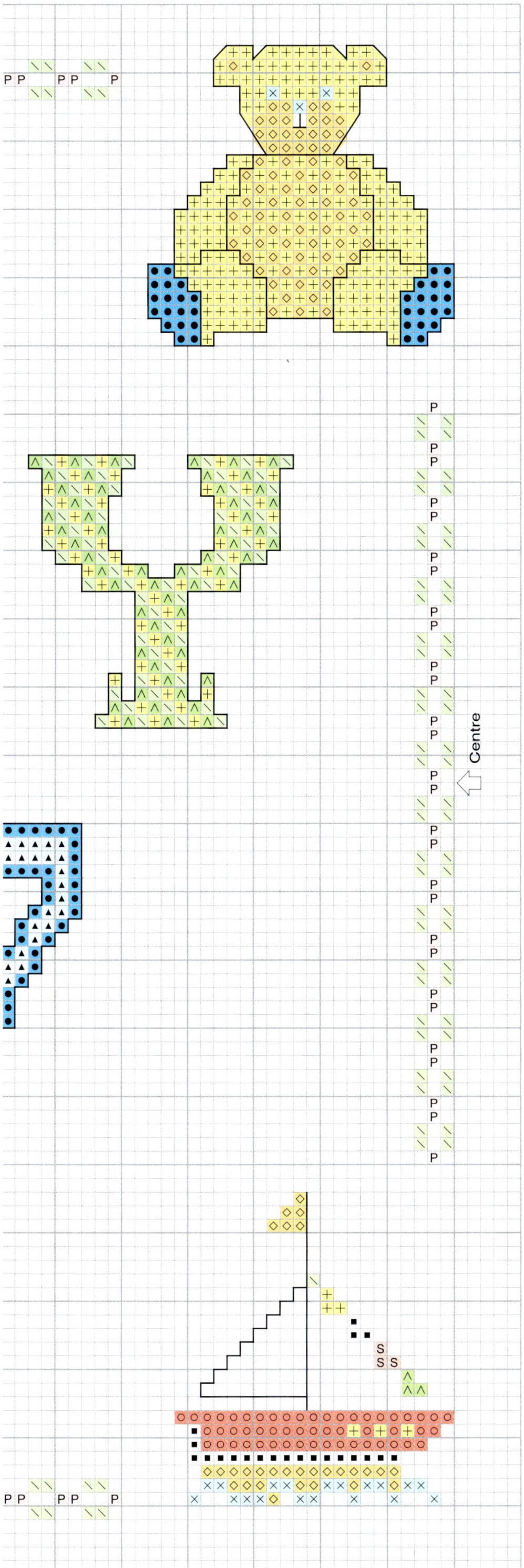

COT SHEET

1 Cut a 65 x 8 cm strip of Aida and overlock the edges to prevent fraying. Find the mid-point of the piece by folding it in half lengthways, then crossways. Mark the vertical and horizontal lines across the mid-point with sewing thread.

2 Work out the placement of the lettering (see pages 90–1), leaving two squares between each letter. It may be necessary to change the colour scheme of some of the letters so as to balance out the colours. Work the letters in cross stitch from the top down, making sure that all your threads cross over in the same direction.

3 Cut a piece of check fabric 120 x 65 cm. Measure 20 cm down from the top of the material and hand baste a strip of piping across, with its rolled edge facing downwards. Use a row of checks to help you place it straight.

4 Place the bottom edge of the embroidered Aida strip right side down along the flat edge of the piping, hand baste together, then machine stitch. Turn the Aida strip right side up.

5 Place a second strip of piping along the top edge of the Aida strip, with the flat edge up and the rolled edge nearest the embroidery. Hand baste, then machine stitch.

6 With the right side of the sheet facing you, measure 1.5 cm from the top edge, fold it in and press. Bring this folded edge to the edge of the piping, so that it covers the flat edge and rests neatly against the rolled edge. Hand baste, then using a zipper foot, machine stitch neatly, close to the folded edge of the check material.

7 Make a narrow hem at the other end of the sheet, then with a 1.5 cm seam allowance make a hem down each side of sheet. To make a matching pillowcase see the instructions for the pillowcase in 'Starry sheet and pillowcase' on page 26.

Each of these cross-stitch letters is outlined in a complementary colour using back stitch.

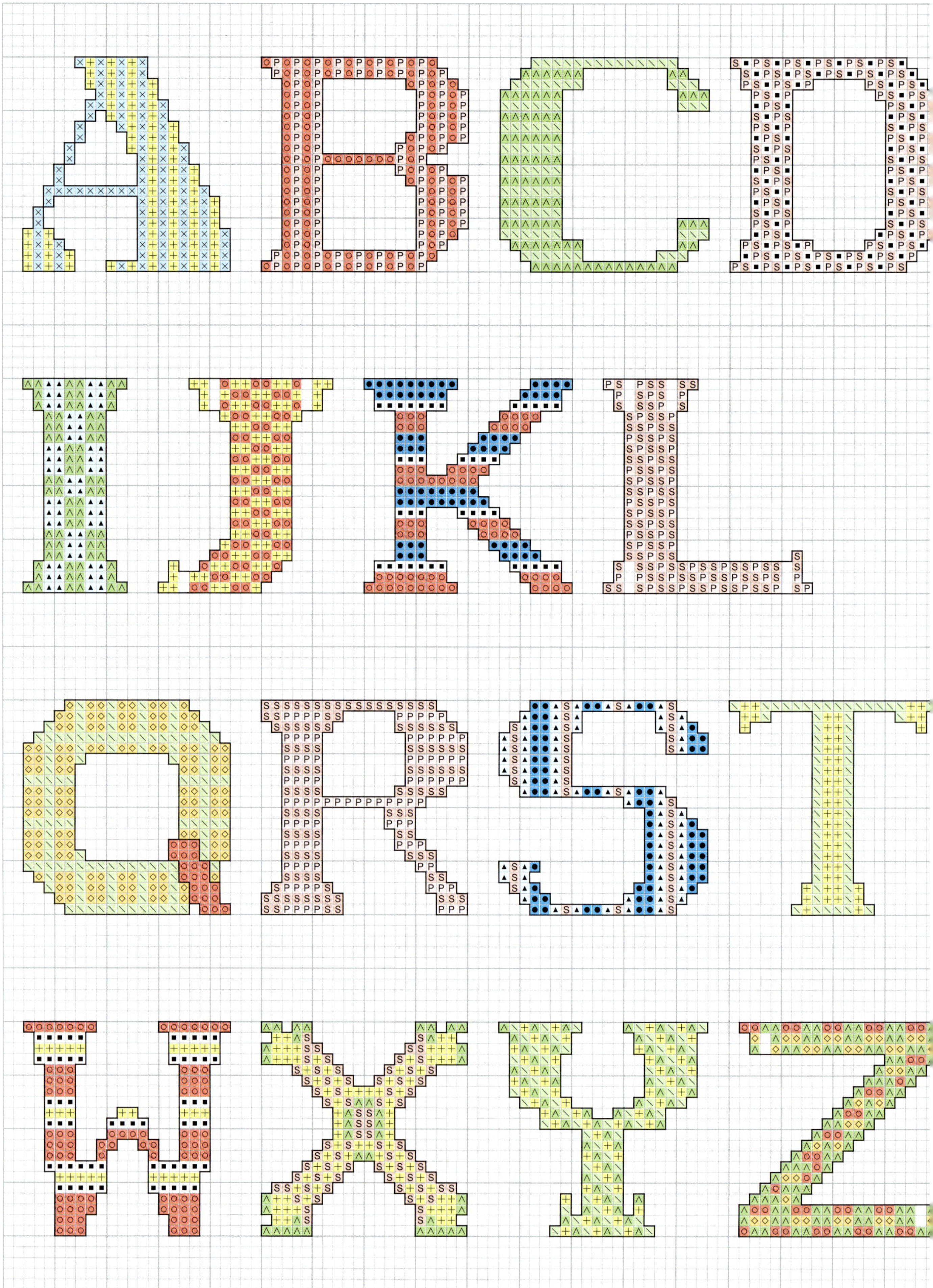

Outline colour key
All letters are outlined in back stitch

A	Dark blue	J	Red	S	Dark blue
B	Red	K	Dark blue	T	Hunter green
C	Hunter green	L	Dark blue	U	Dark blue
D	Dark pink	M	Dark blue	V	Hunter green
E	Dark blue	N	Red	W	Red
F	Hunter green	O	Red	X	Hunter green
G	Dark blue	P	Red	Y	Hunter green
H	Dark blue	Q	Hunter green	Z	Red
I	Hunter green	R	Dark blue		

DMC colour key

●	824	Dark blue
×	809	Medium blue
▲	828	Light blue
o	666	Red
+	973	Yellow
∧	3346	Hunter green
\	3348	Yellow-green
◇	721	Orange
S	602	Dark pink
P	605	Light pink
■	White	

Numbers 0 - 9

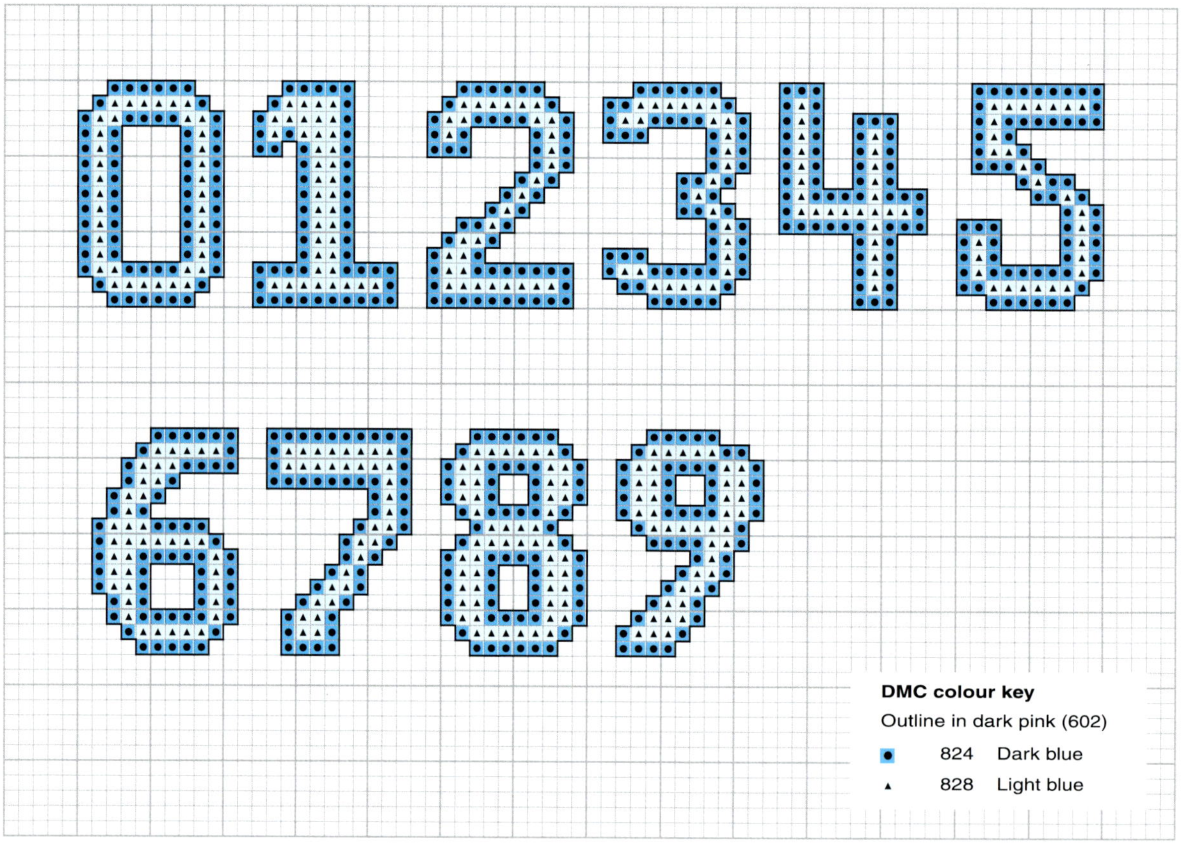

BIB

1 Take the 30 x 5 cm band of Aida and overlock the side edges to prevent fraying. Find the mid-point of the piece by folding it in half lengthways, then crossways. Mark the vertical and horizontal lines across the mid-point with sewing thread.

2 Work out the placement of the lettering, leaving two squares between each letter. It may be necessary to change the colour scheme of some of the letters so as to balance out the colours. Work the letters in cross stitch from the top down, making sure all your threads cross over in the same direction.

3 Use the pattern on page 106 to cut two pieces of check material and one piece of towelling. Hand baste one of the check pieces to the towelling. Working on the right side, pin a strip of piping approximately two-thirds of the way down the bib, with the rolled edge uppermost. Hand baste into place.

4 Place the embroidered Aida band onto the bib, with the top edge resting neatly against the piping. Use it as a guide to hand baste another strip of piping into place, but with its rolled edge facing downwards.

5 With the edges of the Aida band laying perfectly along the flat edge of the piping, use a zipper foot to stitch all the pieces together. To be sure the Aida band is fastened down, make another row of stitching a short distance away.

6 Take the second piece of check material and pin it carefully to the towelling.

7 Open out one of the edges of the bias binding and press. Place the pressed edge of the binding right sides together with the front of the bib. Machine stitch the binding along the edge of the bib, but leave the curved neck area (from * to *) unfinished. Turn to the back of the bib, turn the edge of the binding under and hand stitch neatly.

8 Machine stitch around the edge of the curved neck area to hold the three layers neatly together. Cut a strip of bias binding approximately 75 cm long, open out one of the edges and press. With right sides together, place the pressed edge onto the curved neck area and, ensuring you have left at least 30 cm on either side for tying around baby's neck, hand sew the binding carefully over the machine stitching. Turn to the back of the bib, fold the edge of the binding under and hand sew. Then hand stitch the edges of the ties together, turning the edges and ends under for neatness.

Cutwork coathangers

With their lovely cutwork embroidery and ribbons aplenty, these coathangers are so pretty it will be a shame to hide them in the wardrobe. Show them off by giving them as gifts instead.

Finished size Approximately 43.5 cm long and 16 cm high (maximum measurements)

Stitches

Buttonhole stitch
Chain stitch
Running stitch
Stem stitch

Materials

- 75 cm of white handkerchief linen or similar
- 75 cm of pale floral fabric
- DMC stranded embroidery cotton to match or contrast
- Two plastic-coated wire coathangers
- 30 cm of white felt
- Crewel needle size 10
- 5 mm wide ribbons
- Small beads
- Machine thread to match fabric
- 15 cm (6 in) embroidery hoop
- Sheet of paper approximately 60 x 30 cm (or join two A4 sheets together)
- Stiletto
- Sharp embroidery scissors and HB pencil

PREPARATION

1 Trace the outline of a coathanger onto paper. Measure approximately 1.5 cm seam allowance and leave 4 cm across the bottom edge.

2 Using this template, cut two pieces of felt, continuing only 1 cm into the hook to allow for the bulky joint of wire. Stitch around the shoulders and sides of the felt, leaving the top (the hook opening) and bottom unstitched. Trim the seams to about 5 mm.

Coathanger 1 motif

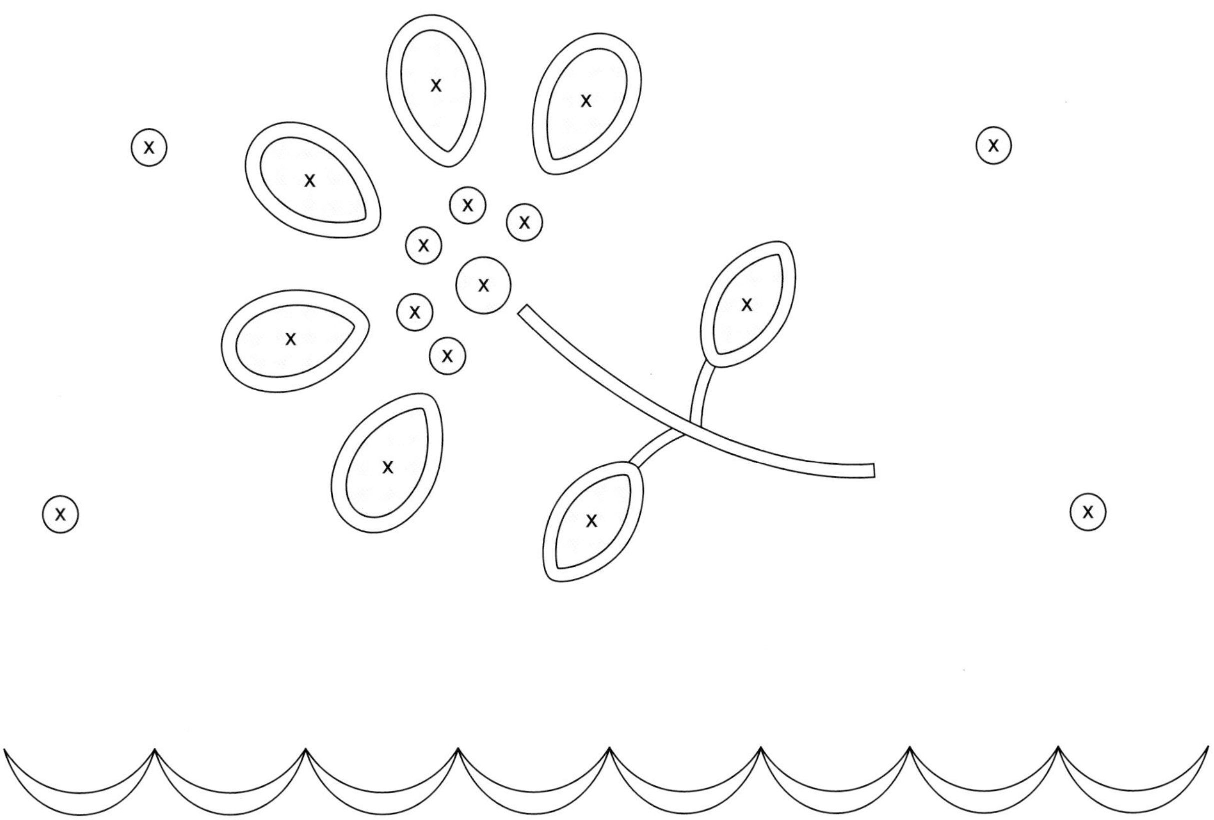

Coathanger 2 motif

3 Place the coathanger inside the felt and hand baste across the bottom, then machine stitch as close to the hanger as possible (use a zipper foot).

EMBROIDERY

1 With a pencil, transfer the embroidery design to the right side of the material, adding scallops right across the bottom. For Coathanger 1, add extra eyelets around the design. On the back indicate only the scallops.

2 Work the coathanger designs as follows:
Coathanger 1. On the white handkerchief linen work the flower's stem in two rows of stem stitch. Chain stitch around the petals, leaves and scallops, then work buttonhole stitch over them, with the edge of the stitches being towards the inside, where the fabric will later be cut away, except for the scallops. For the eyelets (including the flower's centre), work tiny running stitches around the edges, then use a stiletto to make the holes. Finally, overcast the edges.
Coathanger 2. On the floral fabric work the veins of the leaves in stem stitch. Use chain stitch on the remaining outlines (to 'pad' the design), then work over them in buttonhole stitch. Add beads to the centre of each flower for decoration.

3 Using an inconspicuous colour, work a crescent of buttonhole stitches around the mouth through which the hook will pass.

TO FINISH

1 Place the front and back embroidered pieces right sides together and carefully pin, matching the scallops at the sides. Machine stitch the shoulders and sides, leaving the top and bottom open. Trim the seams and turn through to the right side.

2 Using a sharp pair of embroidery scissors, cut out the areas marked 'x' on the design and around the scallops. Press carefully.

3 Place the cover over the prepared hanger and work catch stitch at various points to hold the layers in place. Alternatively, sew a bead at the point of each scallop.

4 Make bows with the ribbons and fasten each at the base of the hook. Trim the bottom of the felt to 5 mm below the scallops.

LEFT It's easy to jazz up your coathangers. With needle and thread and a bit of imagination, you'll have these made in no time.

Tapestry accessories

The captivating tapestry on these accessories is worked entirely in continental stitch, using embroidery wool on mono canvas.

Jazz up your wardrobe with this unique set of accessories. Inspired by ethnic designs and based on the colours of the earth, it will lend the finishing touch to any casual outfit.

Finished size Belt 3.5 x 70 cm including buckle; hat band 2.5 x 60 cm; brooch 5 x 5 cm

Stitches

Continental stitch

Materials

- Mono canvas with 10-count to 1 inch
- DMC Laine Colbert embroidery wool: light yellow (7078), red copper (7449), ochre (7446), orange (7437), dark yellow (7742), green (7386)
- 80 cm of 3.5 cm wide brown corded ribbon
- 60 cm of 2.5 cm wide brown corded ribbon
- Tapestry needle size 24
- Self-closing buckle
- 5 cm square of cardboard or plastic
- 5 cm square of felt
- Brooch back pin
- Brown sewing thread
- PVA adhesive
- Scissors

BELT

This belt is 70 cm long. If you need a longer size, work an extra panel or some plain rows at each end to make the desired length. To shorten, work one panel less and make up any difference by plain rows at the ends. Don't forget to allow for the width of the self-closing buckle.

1 Cut a strip of canvas 8 x 80 cm. Centre the design (see page 98) against the 8 cm side edge to allow for turnings. Embroider the belt in continental stitch following the chart, but at each end work six plain vertical rows of red copper (7449) to attach the wide buckle. When the embroidery is completed, bend any excess canvas over to the back.

2 Sew the 3.5 cm wide ribbon to the back of the belt with small topsewing stitches along the edges.

3 Tuck the ends into the buckle and sew them down neatly and firmly.

HAT BAND

1 Cut a strip of canvas 5 x 60 cm and centre the design (see page 98) against the 5 cm side edge (as for the belt) to allow for turnings. Embroider in continental stitch, following the chart. When completed, bend any excess canvas over to the back.

2 Sew the 2.5 cm wide ribbon onto the back of the hat band, using topsewing stitches.

BROOCH

1 Cut a square of canvas 10 x 10 cm and centre the design (see page 98). Work the embroidery in continental stitch, following the chart.

2 Place the embroidery over the cardboard square, turn back the excess edges and glue down firmly.

3 Glue the felt onto the back of the brooch, trim it to size and stitch around the edges, oversewing with red copper (7449) wool.

4 Glue on the back pin, anchoring it with a few stitches if desired.

RIGHT This attractive belt, hatband and brooch set is easy to make and a pleasure to wear.

Belt

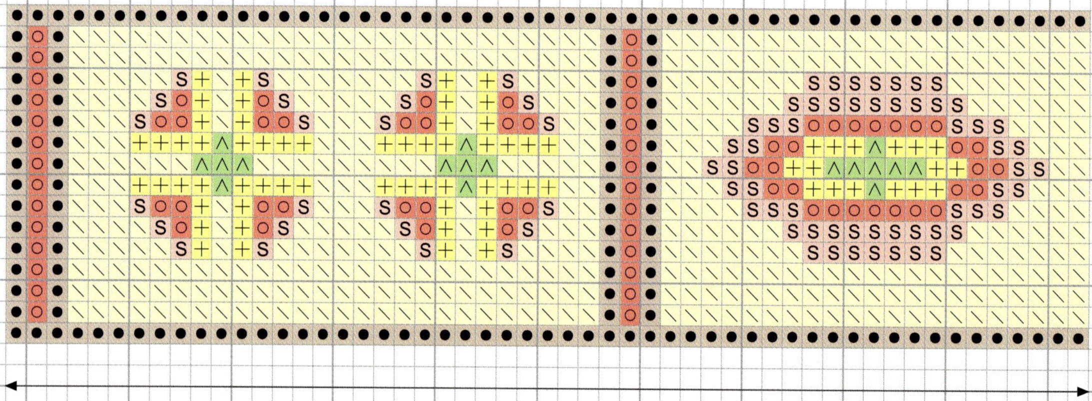

Repeat

Hat band

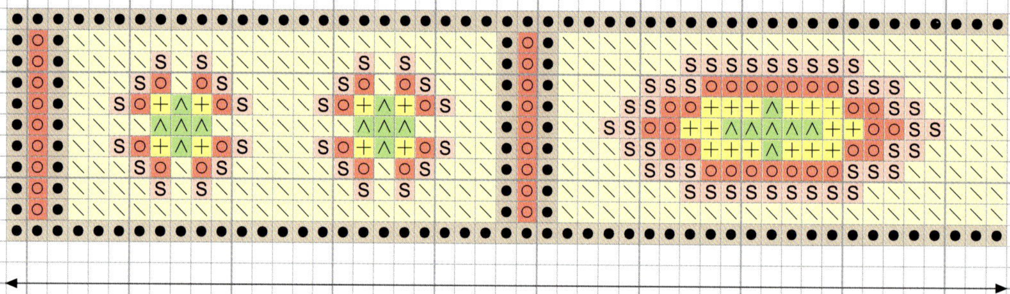

Repeat

Brooch

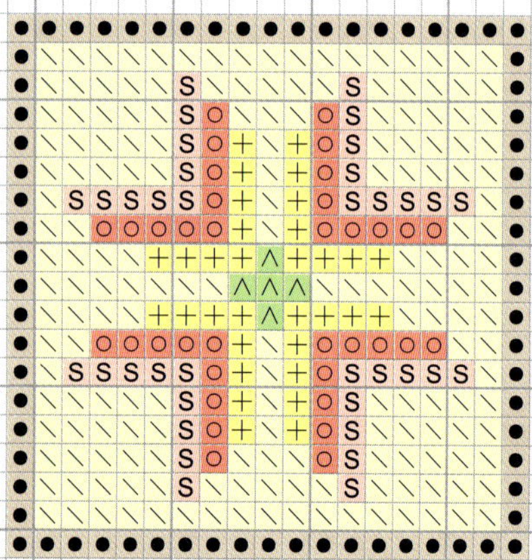

DMC wool colour key

\	7078	Light yellow
●	7449	Red copper
S	7446	Ochre
O	7437	Orange
+	7742	Dark yellow
∧	7386	Green

Smocked Christmas balls

Add a personal touch to your Christmas tree with these handmade smocked balls. They will last a long time and become a Christmas tradition.

Finished size Approximately 25 cm in circumference

Stitches

Back stitch or smocker's knot
Cable stitch
Outline stitch
Two-step wave stitch

Materials

- Three 3-inch polystyrene balls
- 20 cm of lining fabric in each of red, blue and cream
- DMC stranded embroidery cotton: green (500), red (498), white
- Madeira metallic thread: gold (3008), silver (3010)
- Quilting needle size 10
- Four gold and two silver A6 ball caps (The Australian Bead Company)
- Gold and silver filler beads DI 783 (The Australian Bead Company)
- 30 cm of 2 mm wide silver ribbon
- 60 cm of 2 mm wide gold ribbon
- Pleater or smocking transfer dots
- Quality thread matching the fabric as well as a contrast colour
- Pins
- Spray starch
- Scissors

SMOCKING

1 Cut a piece of lining fabric 15 cm wide. Cut off the selvedge and cut the piece 70 cm long. Spray starch the fabric.

2 Pleat the fabric with either a pleater or smocking transfer dots. If you choose the latter, make sure the fabric is absolutely straight. Cut a piece of transfer paper to fit the fabric and line up the dots with the grain on the wrong side of the fabric. Pin and tuck in place. Use an iron set to a low heat to press carefully, and check that the dots are transferred properly. Using a fine needle and contrasting colour thread, gather up the dots. The thread needs to be longer than the width of the fabric to enable you to gather

Christmas ball chart

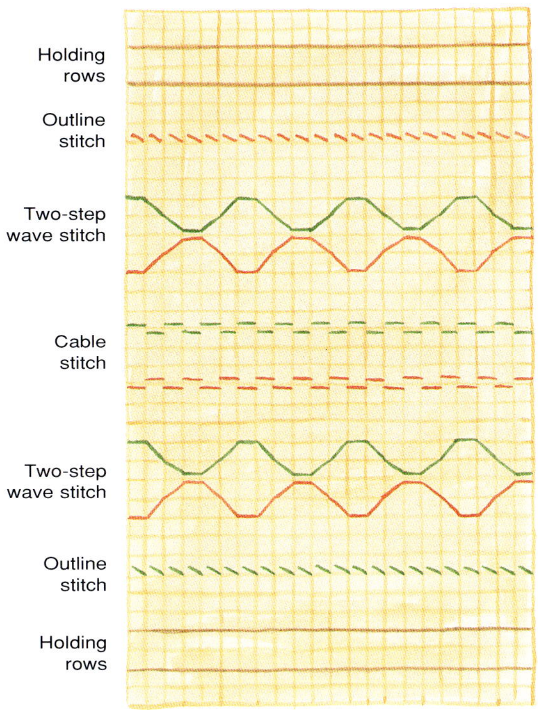

COLOUR KEY

	Cream ball	Blue ball	Red ball
(Outline stitch)	Red	White	Green
(Two-step wave stitch)	Green	Silver	White
	Red	Silver	White
(Cable stitch)	Green	White	Gold
	Red	White	Gold
(Two-step wave stitch)	Green	Silver	Green
	Red	Silver	Green
(Outline stitch)	Green	White	White

Two-step wave stitch (trellis stitch)

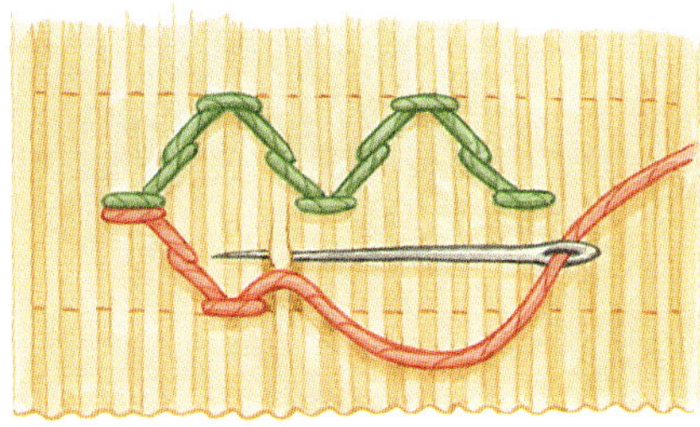

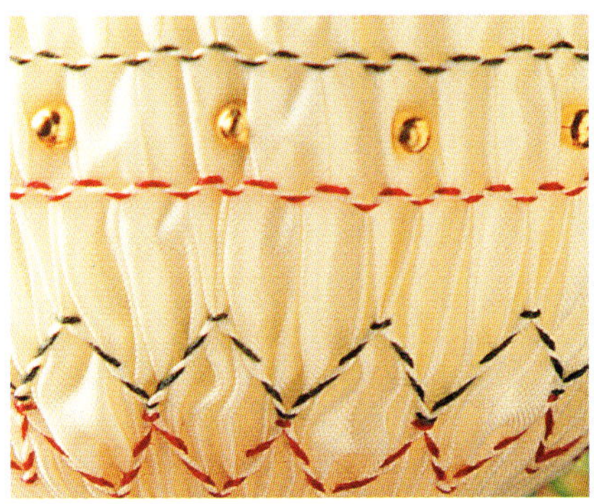

Gold beads add a merry touch to these delightful Christmas balls.

the dots neatly. Pleat 14 full rows, including four holding rows. Pull the threads from the left and knot them together in pairs on the left side. Excluding the holding rows, gather them in a bundle at the other end and trim.

3 Smocking is generally worked from left to right. Before threading your needle, separate the strands of the embroidery thread, then put them together again. The 'dips' between the pleats are called 'valleys'. When you start smocking, put a knot in the end of the thread and come up in the valley next to the pleat you are going to smock. Insert the needle through the first pleat from right to left. This gives you a back stitch and secures the thread. Follow the smocking chart for the embroidery (see page 99). The three balls use the same pattern but different colours.

Blue ball: DMC stranded cotton in white and Madeira silver (3010);

Red ball: DMC stranded cotton in white, green (500) and Madeira gold (3008);

Cream ball: DMC stranded cotton in green (500) and red (498).

4 Thread your needle with two strands of cotton in the correct colour. Use a fairly long piece, so that you do not have to fasten off in the middle of the row. Come up in the second 'valley' and embroider the outline stitch in each pleat. The thread for the outline stitch is always above the needle. Complete the row and fasten off.

5 Work the next line in two-step wave stitch, which is worked up and down between two gathering rows with one stitch halfway up between the rows (see the diagram on page 99). The thread should always be behind, like a tail. Work in zigzag from the top gathering row to the lower row, with the thread above the needle, then up again with the thread below the needle. The second row is embroidered close to the one already completed.

6 The next row is cable stitch, straight stitch worked across two pleats below and above the gathering line. Alternate a 'down' cable when the thread lies below the needle and an 'up' cable when the thread lies above the needle.

7 Repeat the embroidery in the reverse order to finish the piece. To finish off, make a few back stitches in the back of the last pleat or use a smocker's knot.

LEFT Using either a pleater or smocking transfer dots, the fabric is gathered and then smocked to create this wonderful effect.

CONSTRUCTION

1 Remove the gathering threads, except the four holding rows.

2 With right sides together and matching the pattern, stitch down the long side by hand or machine to form a tube. Trim the seam and turn right side out.

3 Slip the polystyrene ball inside the tube. Place a few pins around the centre temporarily.

4 Pull the bottom two gathering threads and draw up tightly. Wrap them around the fabric several times before fastening off securely. Take the pins out and repeat the procedure at the other end. Trim off the excess fabric. Place one ball cap over the raw edges and use pins to hold it in place. Use silver caps for the blue ball and gold ones for the other two.

5 For the top end, make a ribbon loop (use silver for the blue ball, gold for the others) and thread it through the cap. Make a knot inside. If the hole in the cap is not large enough to take the ribbon, use a nail with a slightly bigger circumference to enlarge it. Place the ball cap on the top to cover the raw edges and pin in place.

6 Use pins to secure the filler beads evenly around the centre of the ball.

SUCCESSFUL SMOCKING

- Unless you are an experienced smocker, don't use printed fabric. Apart from hurting your eyesight, it will overpower the smocked effect. If you do want to use a printed fabric, make sure the print is straight on the grain, otherwise the design will appear crooked.
- Always wash the fabric before pleating. This removes any added chemicals or dyes, shrinks the fabric and realigns the weave.
- When working on a very lightweight fabric, spray it lightly with starch and iron it before pleating.
- To keep your needles and pleater in good condition, store them in a dark, dry place to prevent them from rusting.
- Before pleating, run a strip of waxed paper through the pleater to lubricate the needles.
- Keep the needle horizontal as you stitch and pick up one pleat at a time.
- Maintain an even tension as you work the embroidery, tugging each stitch gently up or down as you complete the stitch. If the stitches are too tight, your work will lack elasticity.

Cross-stitch Christmas

A touch of metallic gold thread gives the perfect finish to these cross-stitch Christmas accessories. The motifs can also be used for making embroidered Christmas cards.

These Christmas buttons, earrings and brooch are not only easy to make—they're also loads of fun to wear. They're the perfect way to spread a little Christmas cheer.

Finished sizes Buttons 3 cm diameter; earrings 2.5 cm diameter; brooch 4 cm diameter

Stitches

Cross stitch

Materials

- Five 29 mm self-cover button moulds
- Earring mount
- Seven 6 cm squares of 18-count white Aida cloth
- 10 cm square of 18-count white Aida cloth for brooch
- DMC stranded embroidery cotton: bright red (666), green (701), dark green (895), electric blue (995), topaz (725), dark topaz (782)
- Kreinik Balger metallic thread in gold
- Tapestry needle size 24
- Approximately 20 cm of gold cord

- Circle of cardboard or plastic 4 cm in diameter
- Five small red beads
- Small piece of felt
- Brooch pin
- Padding (optional)
- Fray Stop or colourless nail polish
- PVA adhesive

BUTTONS AND EARRINGS

1 Following the chart, embroider each motif in the centre of a 6 cm Aida square. Work each one in cross stitch over one square of fabric using two strands of embroidery cotton.

2 Cut a circle around the embroidery following the instructions given on the button mould or earring mount packaging.

3 Lightly touch the edges of the circle with Fray Stop or colourless nail polish and follow the assembly instructions on the package.

BROOCH

1 Following the chart, embroider the motif in the centre of the 10 cm Aida square. Work the motif in cross stitch over one square of fabric using two strands of embroidery cotton.

2 When the embroidery is complete, add the beads to the holly berries and bell clappers.

3 Cut a circle around the embroidery large enough to cover the cardboard or plastic circle and to overlap on the back. Lightly touch the edges with Fray Stop or colourless nail polish.

4 Work running stitches around the edge of the embroidered circle and place this circle over the cardboard (you may want to add padding at this point). Pull the running stitches gently so as to gather the fabric around the cardboard.

5 Glue a circle of felt on the back of the brooch and glue on the brooch pin.

6 Apply adhesive to the edge of the brooch and glue on a strip of gold cord to neaten the edges.

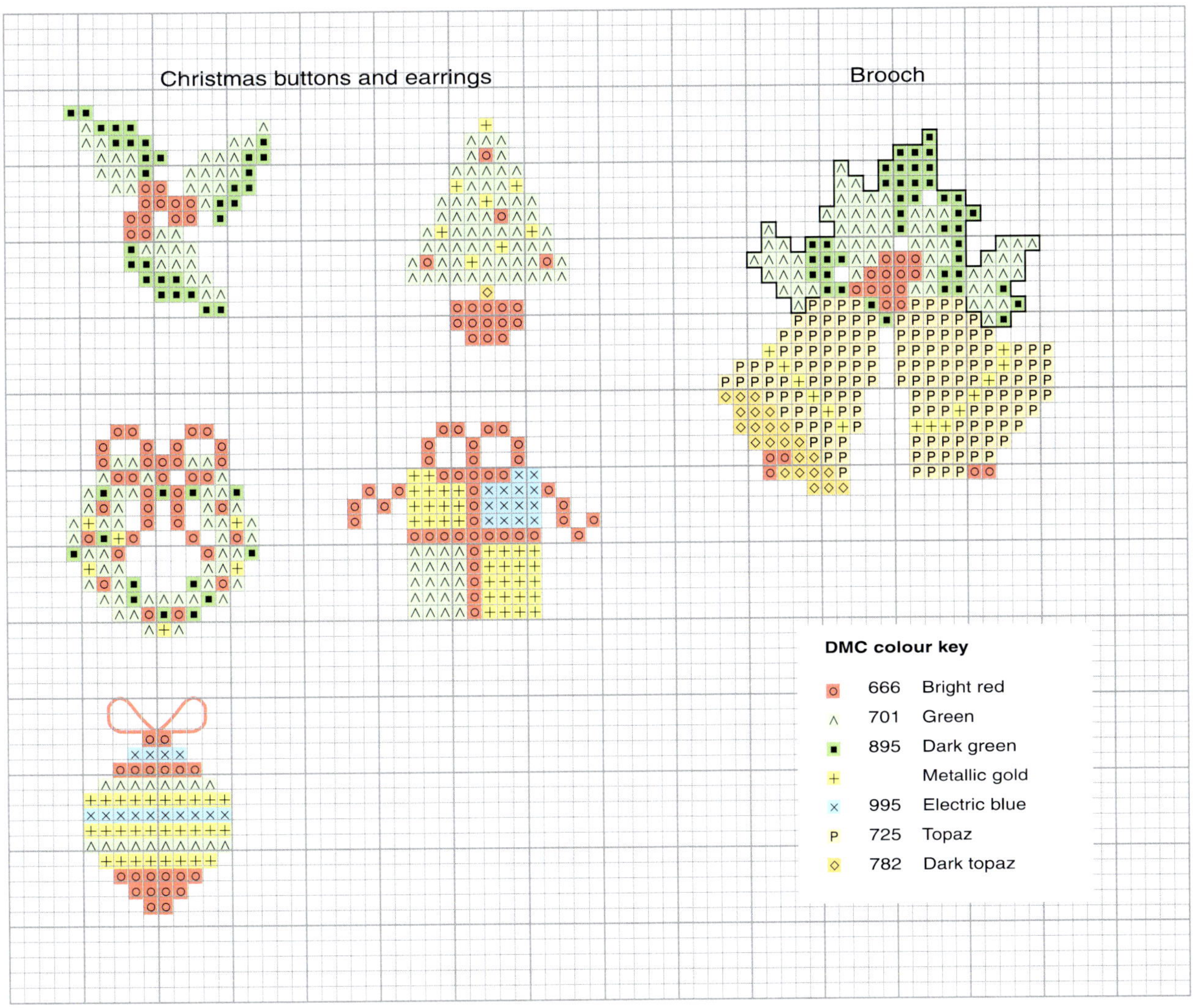

Silken rose sachets and shoe stuffers (page 4)
Shoe stuffer pattern

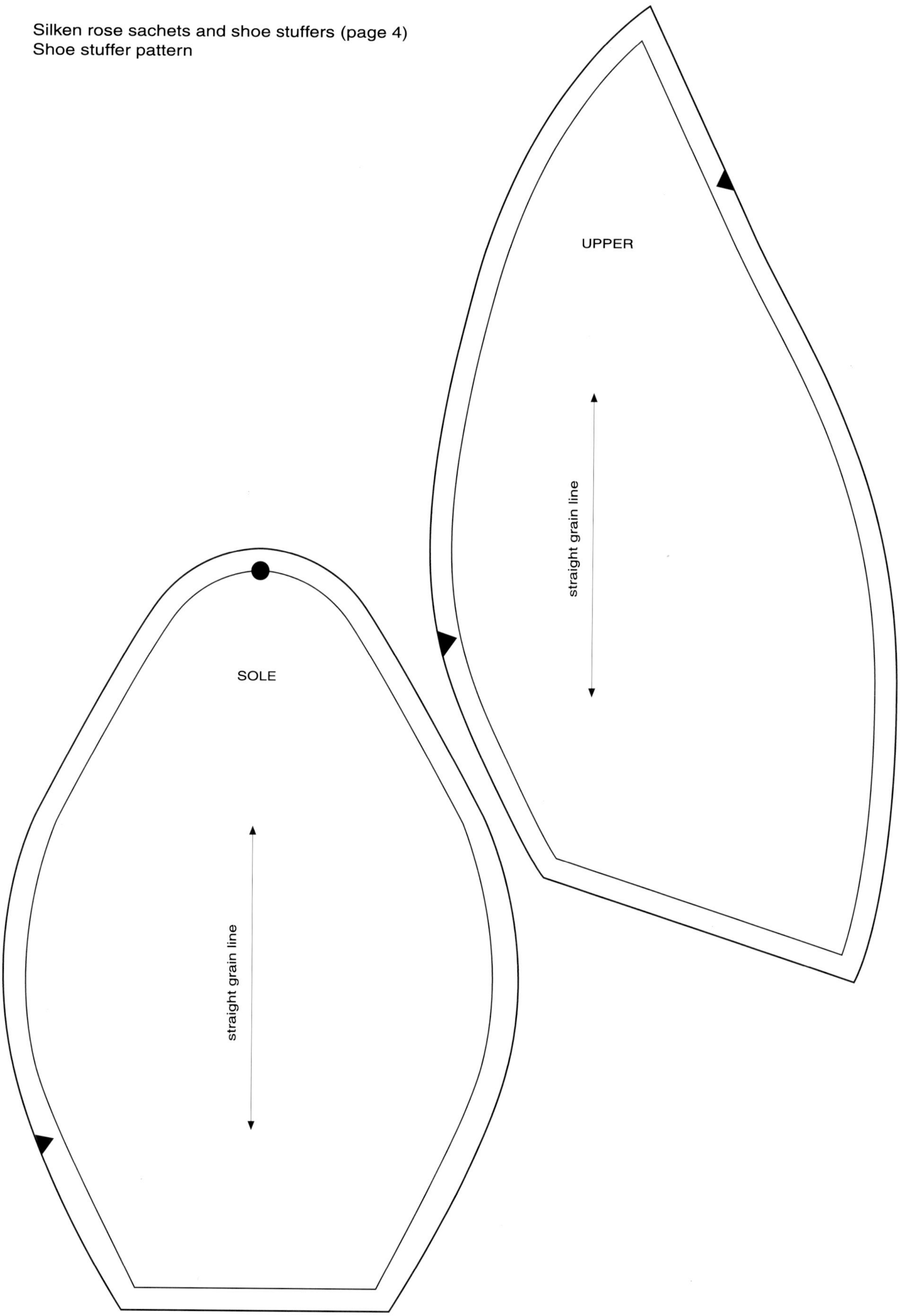

White wedding (page 58)
Wedding pouch pattern

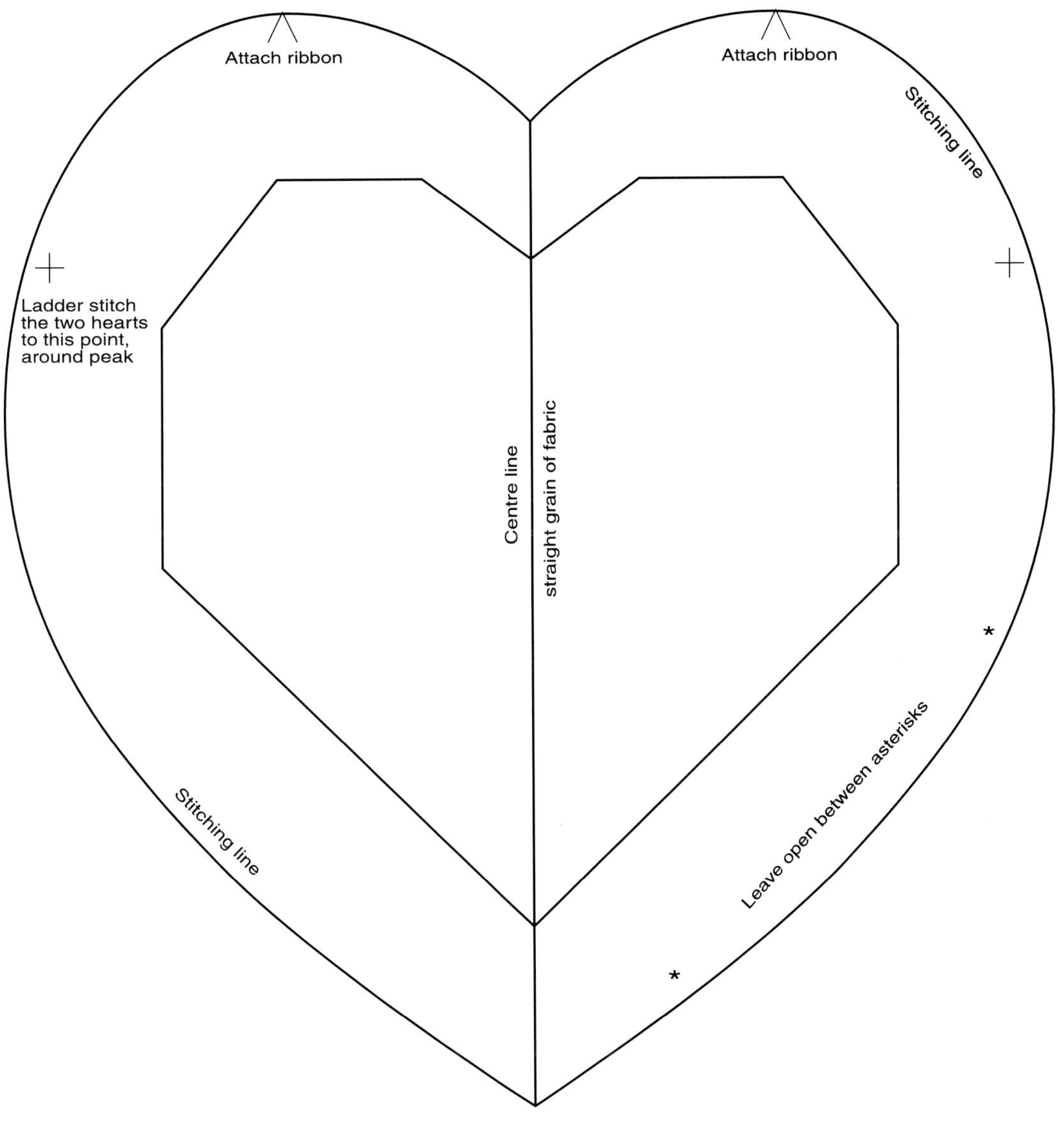

Cross-stitch baby set (page 86)
Bib pattern

Stitch library

Algerian eyelet (star stitch)

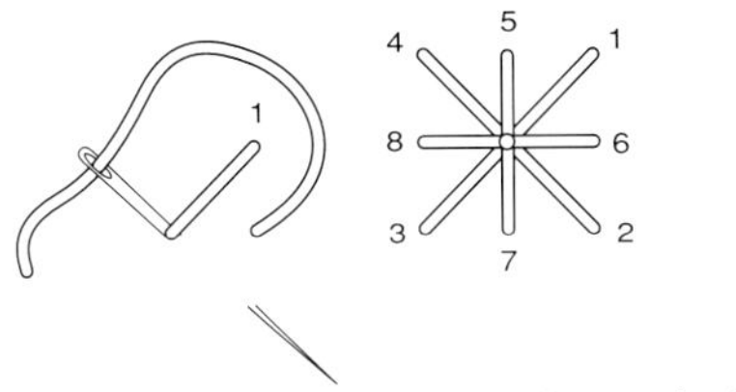

1 Bring needle up at centre and down at 1.

2 Work the required number of stitches.

Blanket stitch

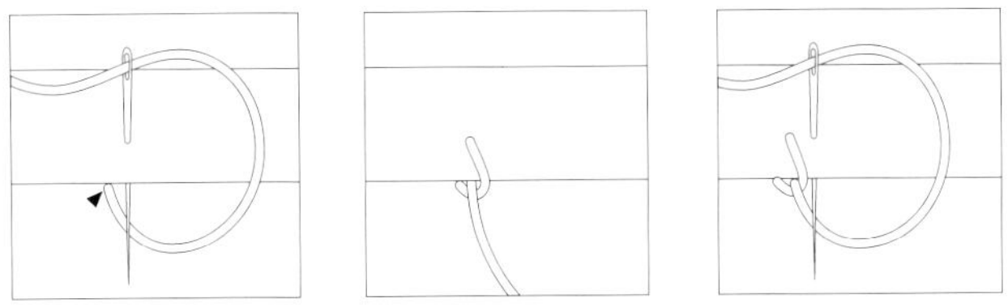

1 Bring thread up at fold, then make a stitch.

2 Pull thread gently.

3 Repeat the stitch, spacing the stitches evenly and ensuring the thread is under the needle.

Bullion stitch

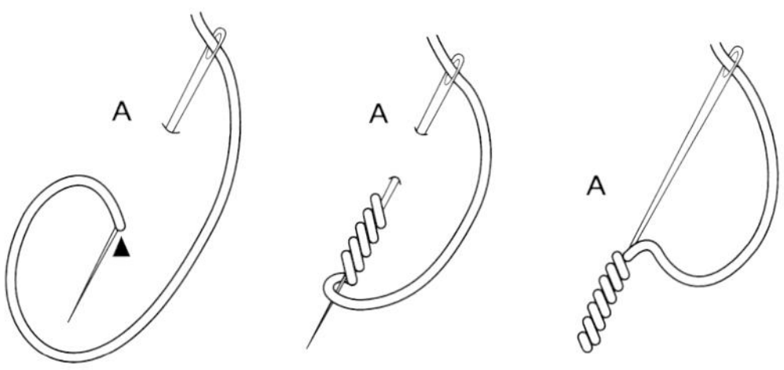

1 Pick up fabric the size of the knot.

2 Twist thread around needle.

3 Pull needle through and insert again at A.

Buttonhole stitch

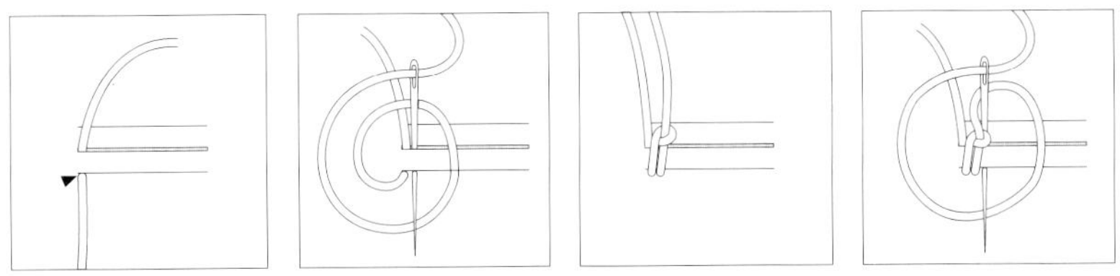

1 Pass needle through opening and up through lower line.

2 Ensure thread is behind needle and insert needle through lower line.

3 Pull thread.

4 Repeat from Step 2.

Cable stitch

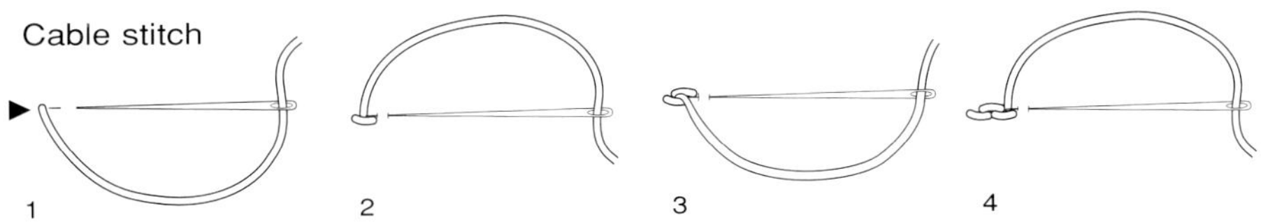

Chain stitch

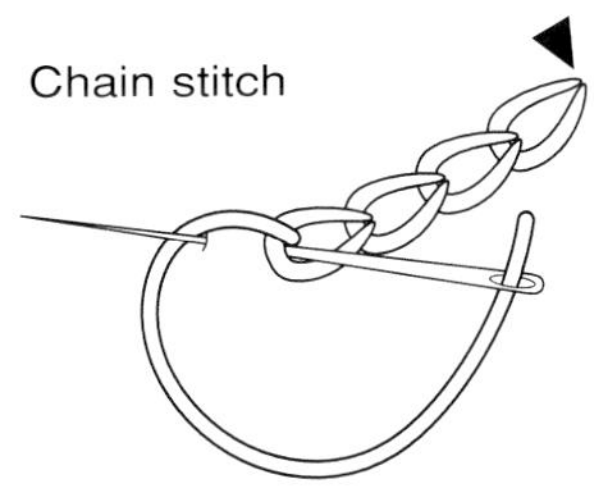

Colonial knot

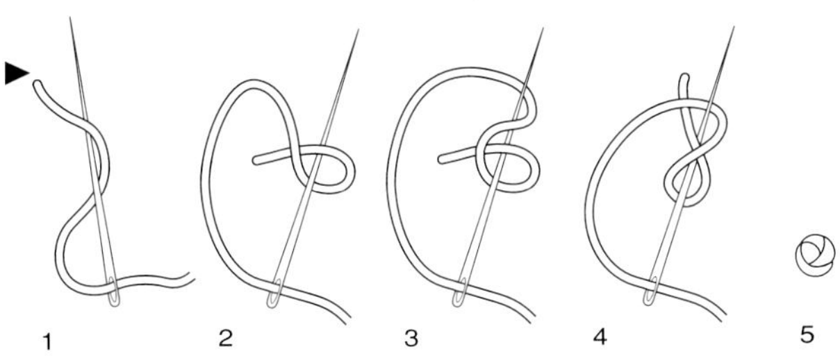

Continental stitch

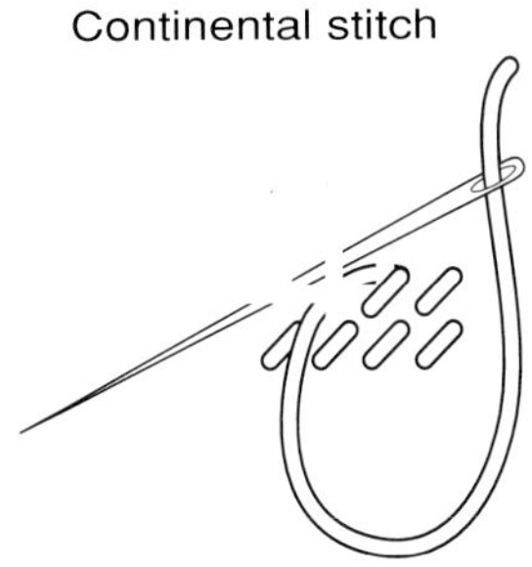

Cross stitch

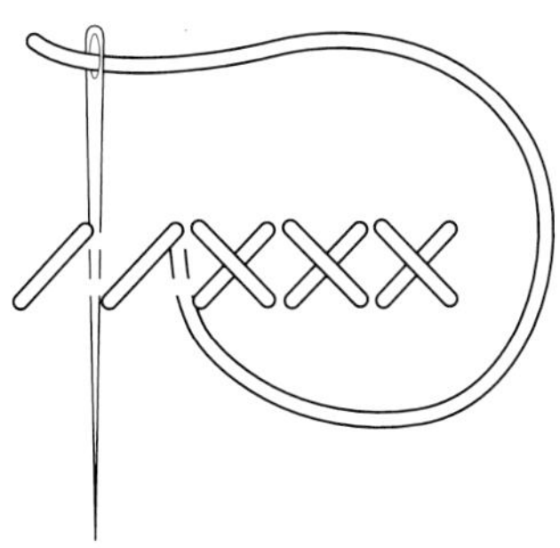

Detached chain stitch (lazy daisy)

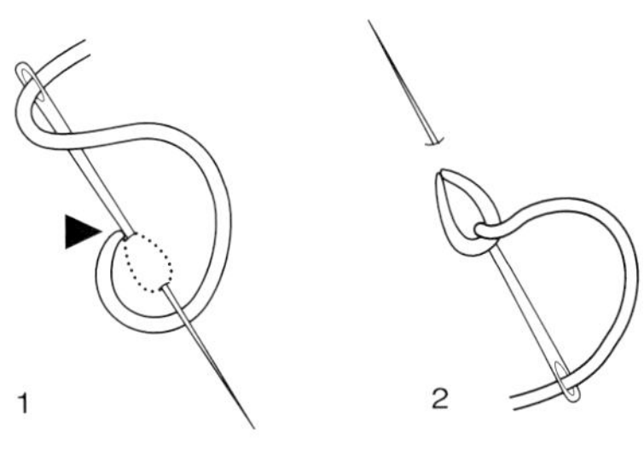

Double back stitch (shadow stitch)

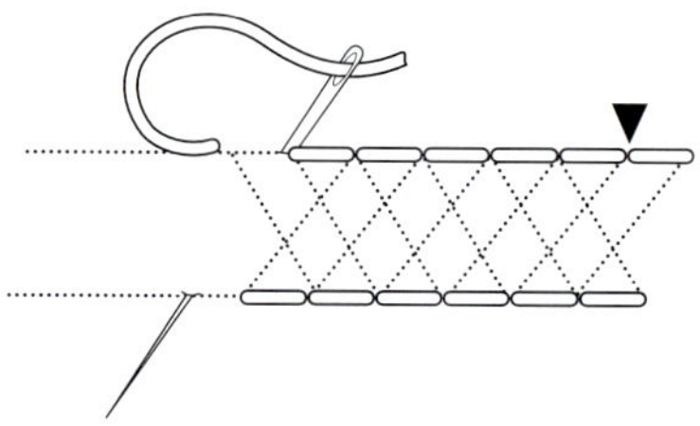

Feather stitch

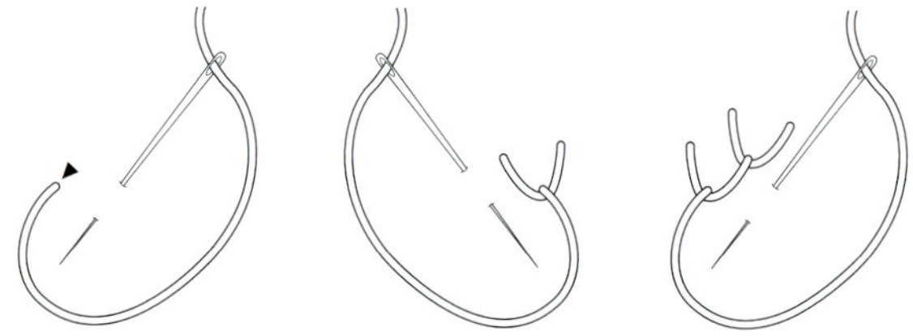

1 Keep the distance between each point the same.

2 Reverse direction of needle for each stitch.

3

Fly stitch

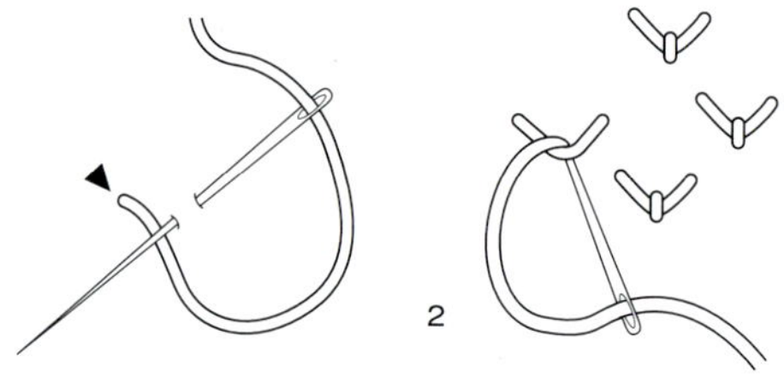

1 2

French knot

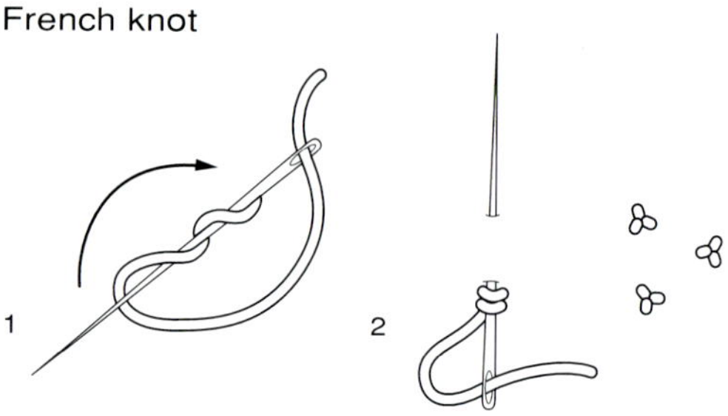

1 2

Four-sided stitch

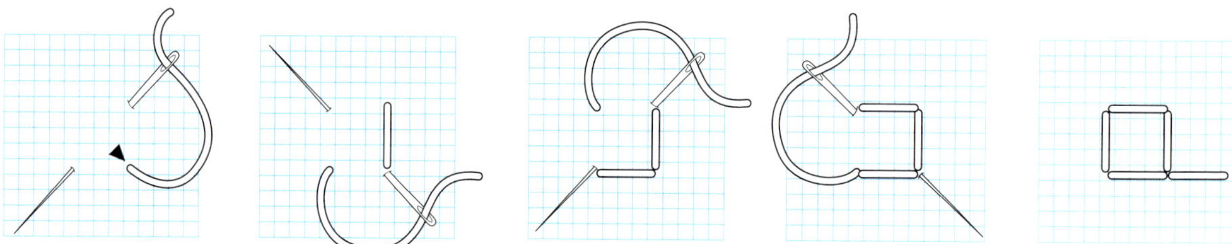

1 2 3 4 5

Hem stitch

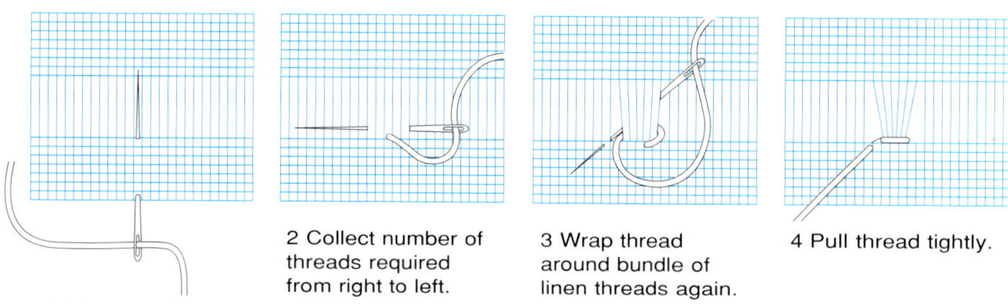

1 Bring needle up on upper fold of hem and secure with a back stitch.

2 Collect number of threads required from right to left.

3 Wrap thread around bundle of linen threads again.

4 Pull thread tightly.

Holbein stitch

1 Work one row of running stitches, leaving two fabric threads between each stitch.

2 Turn fabric upside down and bring needle up on left side of previous stitch.

3 Bring needle down just above end of next running stitch, through same hole in fabric.

4 Repeat, working a new row of stitches.

Ladder hem stitch

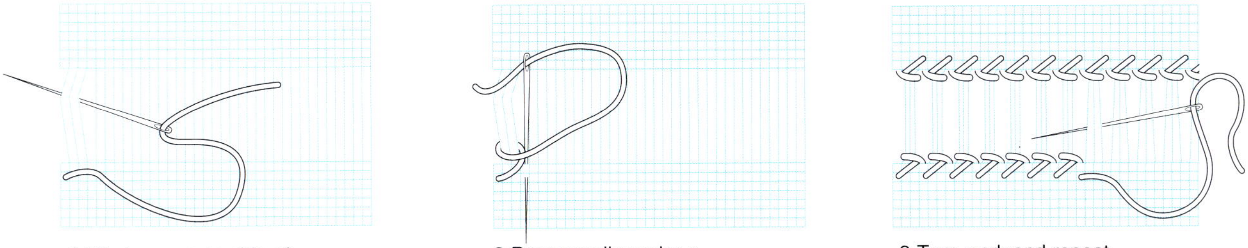

1 Work on wrong side of fabric, from left to right.

2 Pass needle under a few threads.

3 Turn work and repeat.

Ladder stitch

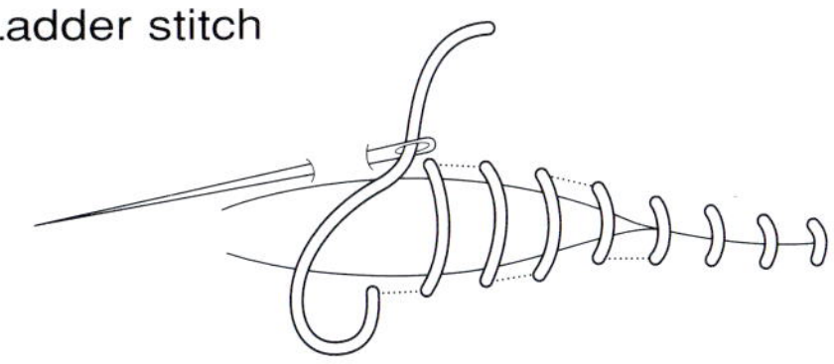

Long and short stitch

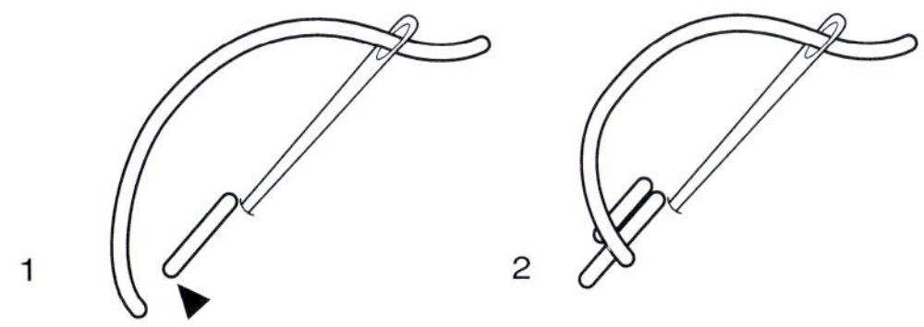

Long-legged cross stitch

1 2 3 4 5

Nun's stitch (open-sided square stitch)

1 2 3 4

Outline stitch

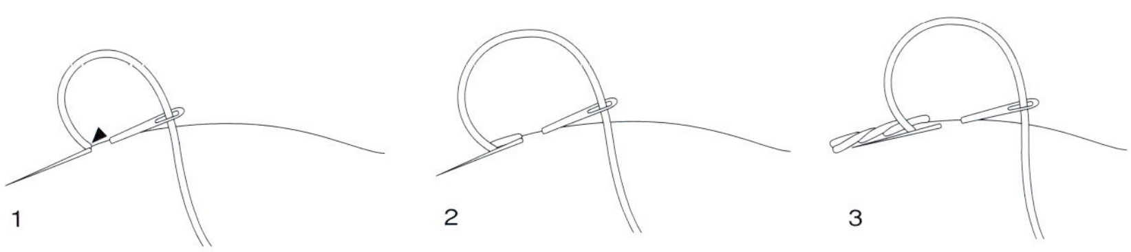

Rosette chain stitch

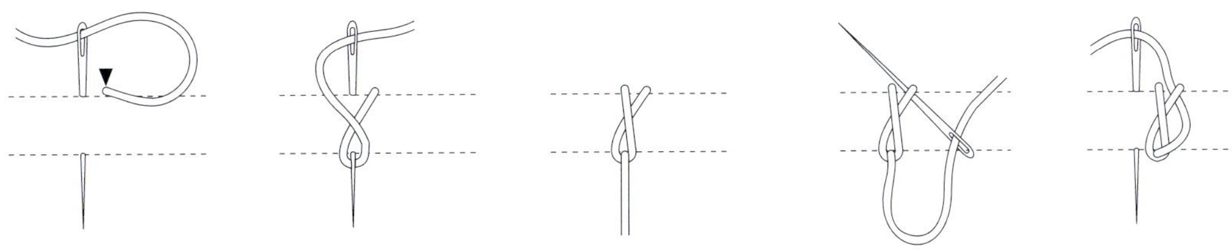

1 Bring needle up, then make a stitch the required length.

2 Wrap thread around needle and pull loop tightly, holding it in place with thumb.

3 Pull thread through.

4 Slide needle under thread and pull thread through.

5 Repeat from Step 1.

Running stitch

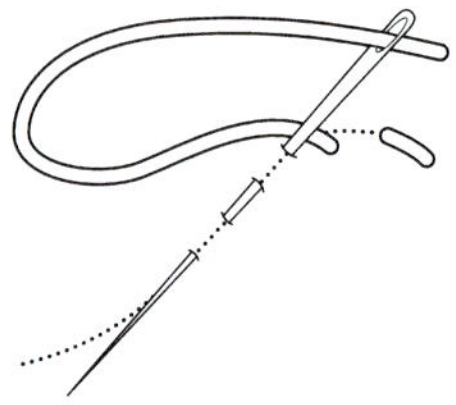

Satin stitch

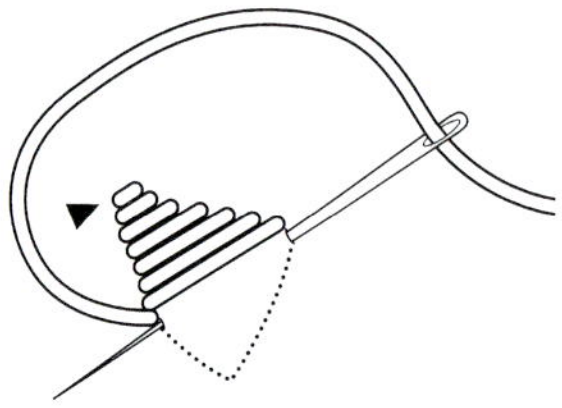

Shell stitch

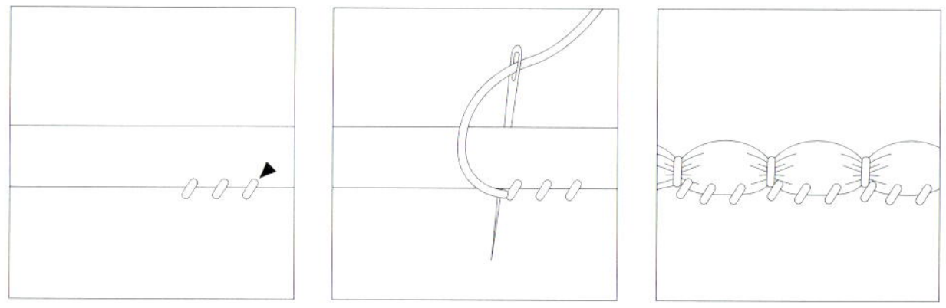

1 Work three small hem stitches.

2 Take needle behind fabric and through close to third stitch. Pull thread firmly but carefully.

3 Continue to form scalloped edge.

Smocker's knot

1 Back stitch.

2 Pull thread leaving a loop.

3 Pass needle through loop to leave a second loop.

4 Pull thread so that first loop is tight and flat.

5 Pass needle through loop.

6 Pull thread tightly and take needle to back.

Smyrna cross stitch

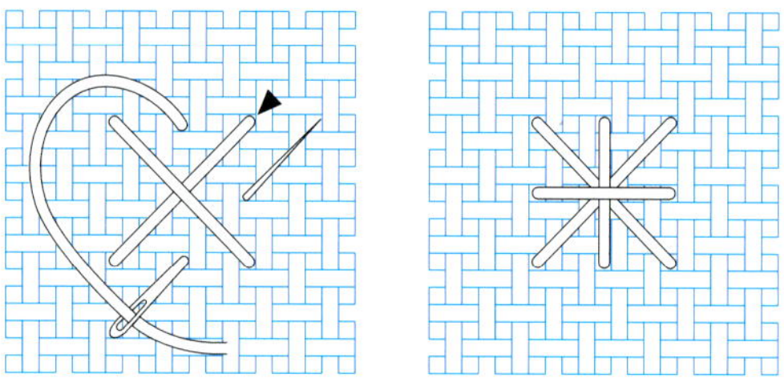

1

2

Split stitch

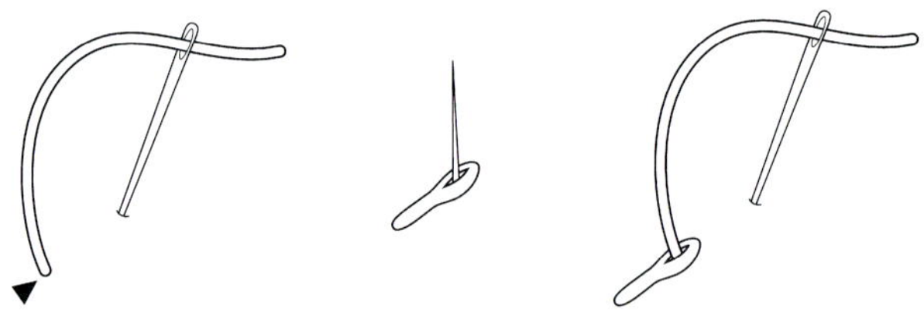

1

2

3

Stab stitch

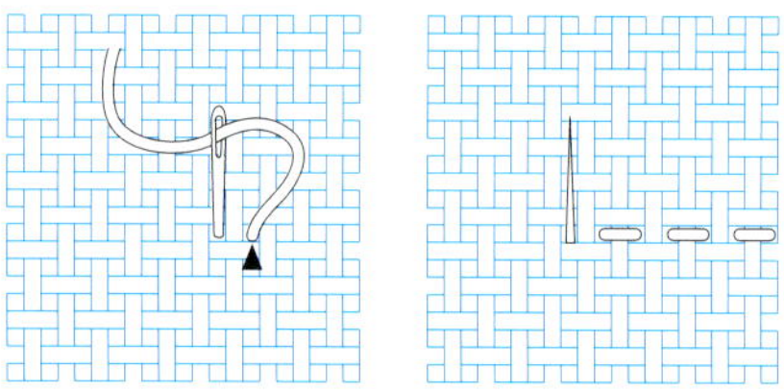

1 Take needle through hole vertically.

2 Continue working with needle perpendicular to fabric.

Stem stitch

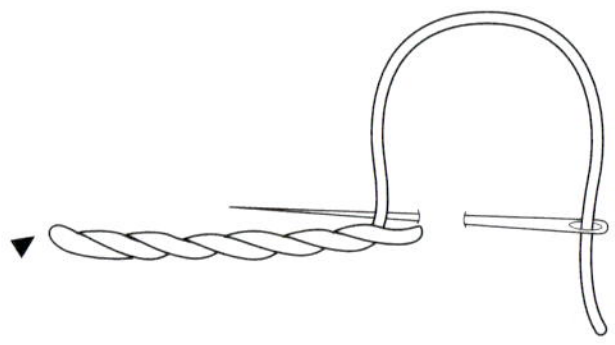

Straight stitch

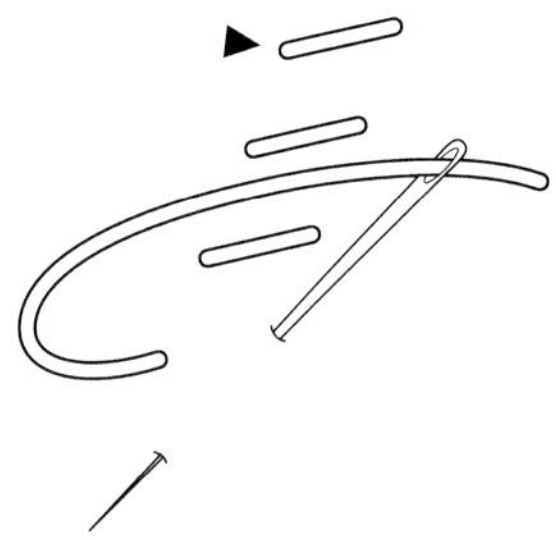

Tent stitch

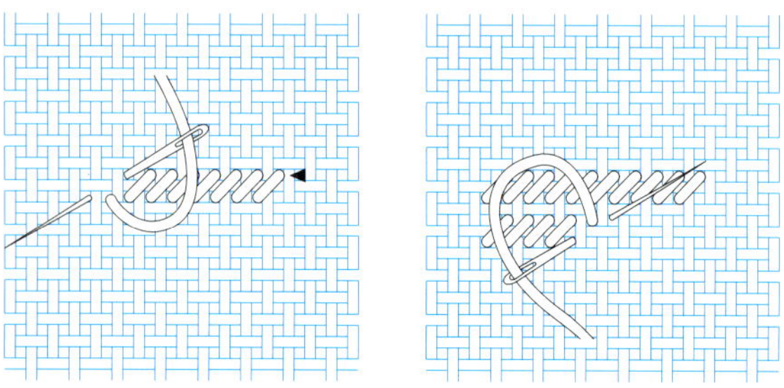

1

2

Wheat stitch

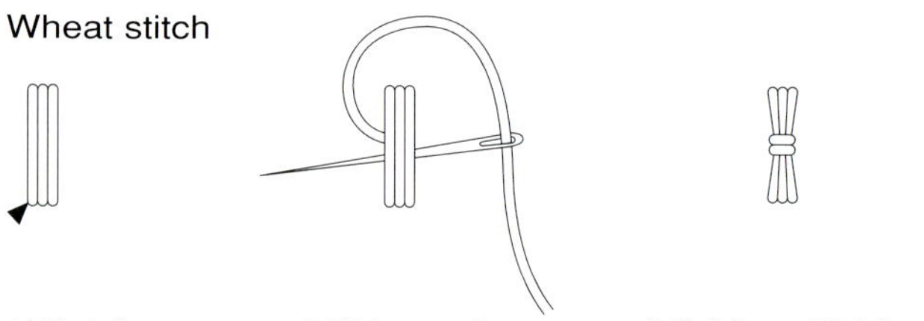

1 Work three vertical stitches side by side.

2 Without going through fabric, pass needle under three stitches.

3 Pull thread tightly and pass needle under stitches again, pulling thread.

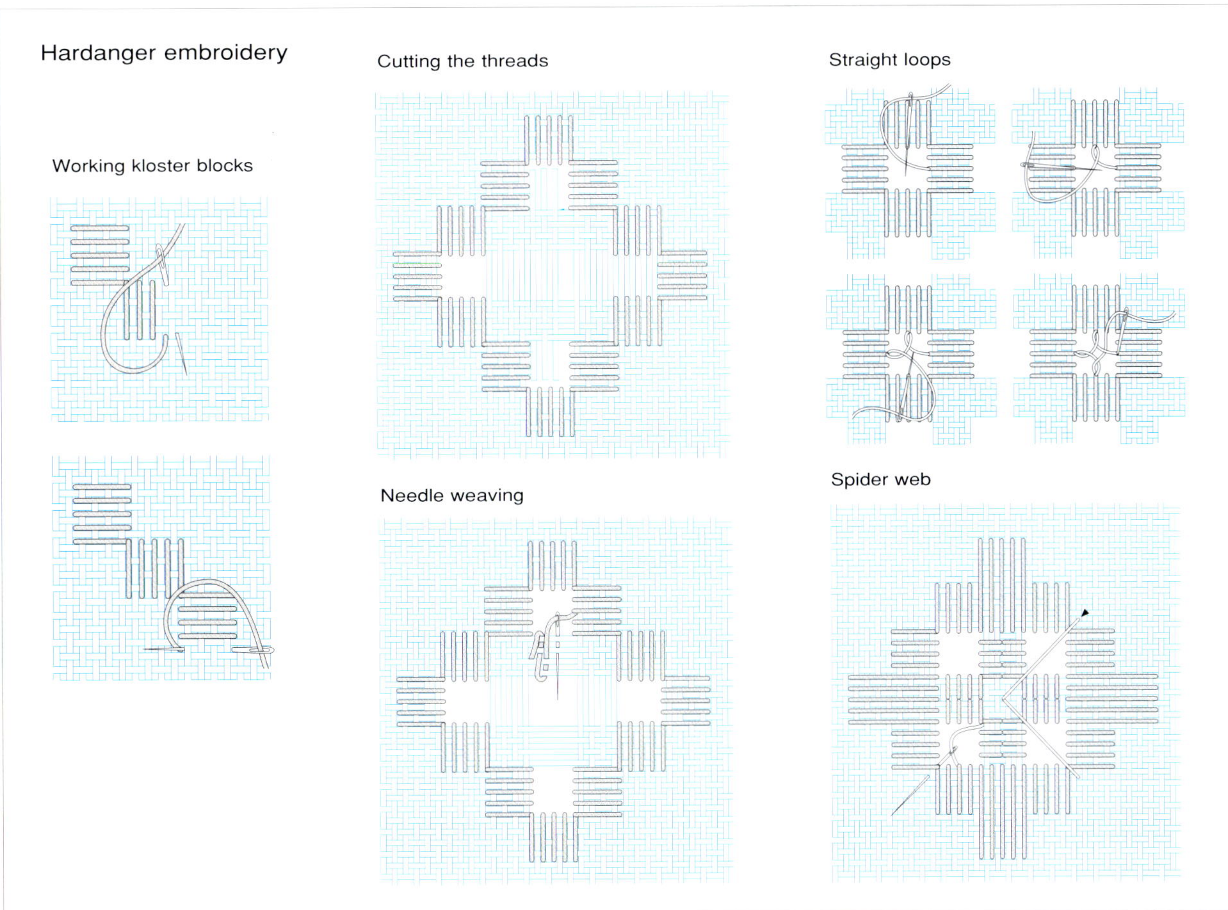
Hardanger embroidery
Working kloster blocks
Cutting the threads
Straight loops
Needle weaving
Spider web

Index

Published by Murdoch Books®, a division of Murdoch Magazines Pty Ltd,
45 Jones Street, Ultimo NSW 2007

Managing Editor, Craft & Gardening: Christine Eslick
Editor: Romina Chapnik
Designer: Wing Ping Tong
Photographer: Andre Martin
Stylists: Kathy Tripp; Lisa Hilton
Illustrators: Stephen Pollitt; Sonya Naumov
Projects designed and made by Bonnie Arthurson, pp. 40, 58, 66, 73 (lavender shadow work), 74; Jennifer Campbell, pp. 8, 15, 26, 69 (yellow roses bag); Phyllis Close, pp. 12, 46, 70 (cutwork sachet); Jenny Jansen, pp. 4, 21, 34, 51, 63, 72 (gum blossoms on organza), 81, 86, 93; Ragnhild Rees, pp. 18, 30, 42, 99; Stella Robinson, pp. 71 (gingham potpourri bag), 78, 96, 102

CEO & Publisher: Anne Wilson
International Sales Director: Mark Newman

National Library of Australia
Cataloguing-in-Publication Data
Beautiful embroidery. Includes index. ISBN 0 86411 841 4
1. Embroidery. 2. Embroidery - Patterns. I. Title: Better Homes and Gardens (North Sydney, N.S.W.). 746.44

Printed by Prestige Litho, Queensland
PRINTED IN AUSTRALIA

First published 1999

Acknowledgements
The publisher would like to acknowledge the following for assistance with photography: Flash Trash, Camperdown; Linen & Lace, Balmain; Roseville Cottage; and Tonbridge Antiques, Roseville.

Every effort has been made to ensure the availability of materials in this book, but the availability of particular colours and fabrics cannot be guaranteed.